Revival
of the
Fittest

Revival of the Fittest

Why Good Companies Go Bad

and

How Great Managers Remake Them

Donald N. Sull

HARVARD BUSINESS SCHOOL PRESS

Boston, Massachusetts

Library of Congress Cataloging-in-Publication Data

Sull, Donald N. (Donald Norman)
    Revival of the fittest: why good companies go bad and how great managers
remake them / Donald N. Sull.
        p.   cm.
    Includes index.
    ISBN 1-57851-993-4 (alk. paper)
    1. Organizational change. 2. Organizational effectiveness. 3. Corporate
image. I. Title.
    HD58.8 .S85 2003
    658.4'06—dc21

                                                                2002154820

To Theresa, Charles, Phillip,
Elizabeth, and Genevieve

CONTENTS

ACKNOWLEDGMENTS

THIS BOOK IS the culmination of hundreds of discussions, questions, and arguments with scholars, students, and managers over the span of a decade. I had the great good fortune of receiving my M.B.A. and doctorate at Harvard Business School, which hosts one of the most vibrant communities of management scholars in the world. My doctoral dissertation committee, chaired by Joseph L. Bower, included George P. Baker, Richard E. Caves, and Nitin Nohria. Together they shaped my thinking on inertia in ways that I may never understand but fully appreciate. Other colleagues at Harvard Business School who helped me design, execute, and make sense of my research include Carliss Y. Baldwin, Christopher A. Bartlett, Henry W. Chesbrough, Clayton M. Christensen, Linda A. Cyr, Thomas R. Eisenmann, David A. Garvin, Clark G. Gilbert, Morten T. Hansen, Robert F. Higgins, Dorothy A. Leonard, Michael E. Porter, John A. Quelch, Jan W. Rivkin, Richard S. Rosenbloom, William A. Sahlman, Alvin J. Silk, Howard H. Stevenson, Richard S. Tedlow, Mary Tripsas, Michael L. Tushman, Richard E. Walton, Jonathan West, and Robert C. Wood. These colleagues' personal guidance, advice, and questions directly influenced my research. The Division of Research at Harvard Business School generously funded my research and I am most grateful for the support. I thank Masako Egawa of Harvard Business School's Japan Research Office, who helped me arrange and conduct interviews with Japanese executives. I also gratefully acknowledge the many managers who generously gave their time and wisdom to bridge the gap from interesting research to practical tools. To paraphrase the African proverb, it takes a village to write a book.

At the London Business School, my good friends and mentors Sumantra Ghoshal, Dominic Houlder, Constantinos C. Markides, and John Stopford provided warm encouragement and cold criticism in just the right mixture. The students in my elective course on inertia and transformation helped refine and deepen my insights. I am particularly grateful to the London Business School students with whom I had the opportunity to collaborate on case studies and master's and doctoral theses, including Simon Andrews, Simoni Angelides, Sam Baker, Jorge Cabrera, Pierpaolo Coda, Richard Coffey, Marcela Escobari, Martin Escobari, Nadine F. Garrido, Beatriz Guimaraes, Elisabeth D. Hoffman, Lee Ji-Hwan, Tobias Kretschmer, Tracey Luke, Junko Matsumi, Moses Ojeisekhoba, Jyoti Rahi, Eduardo Sattamini, Amitabh Sharma, Misha Shukov, Takayuki Sugata, Sandor Talas, Eduardo Tubosaka, and Nigel Turner. I am deeply indebted to a series of able research assistants, including Chris Allen, Chris Choi, Ruchika Dhadwal, Andrew M. Murphy, Emily J. Thompson, and especially Harry Wang. Rafe Sagalyn helped distill the central message of the book and provided sound advice through the long process of writing it.

In conducting this research, it has been a tremendous pleasure to collaborate with and discuss my research with scholars around the world, particularly Carlos Arruda of the Fundação Dom Cabral (Brazil); Robert Burgelman and Kathleen M. Eisenhardt of Stanford; Park Choelsoon of Seoul National University; Michael A. Cusumano of M.I.T.; Yves L. Doz of INSEAD; Kim Ki-Chan of Catholic University of Seoul; Tomo Noda of Institute of Strategic Leadership (Japan); Andrew M. Pettigrew of the University of Warwick; Sirh Jin-Young of the Centerworld Institute of Management

Research (South Korea); Gabriel Szulanski of the Wharton School; and Tom Wylonis of the Scandinavian International Management Institute (Denmark).

I owe a special debt of gratitude to three women. Maurie SuDock diligently assisted in typing and proofreading multiple iterations of the manuscript. Kirsten Sandberg, my editor at Harvard Business School Press, convinced me to write the book in the first place and provided invaluable assistance, editorial advice, and good cheer throughout the process. Above all, I thank my wife, Theresa, who along with our children, Charlie, Phillip, Elizabeth, and Genevieve, made the whole effort worthwhile.

THIS BOOK IS ABOUT managerial commitments—specifically, about making, renewing, and transforming the decisions that determine a company's future path. To succeed in business, every manager must make choices and take actions that may eventually hinder as well as help the organization. As circumstances change, the manager must also change these commitments to continue thriving. A manager's commitments—such as investing financial resources, signing contracts, making public promises, and entering into customer relationships—bind the organization to a future course of action. These commitments enable managers to achieve results, but they also constrain the organization in the future. The central message of this book is simple: Commitments are both a servant and a master.

Not surprisingly, *commitments matter*. We all know that great companies excel in part because founders and subsequent generations of managers make bold commitments. Entrepreneurs as diverse as Laura Ashley, Steve Jobs, and Harvey Firestone rose above their contemporaries by committing to an innovative set of strategies, processes, resources, relationships, and values that defined their organizations' characters. I call this bundle of defining commitments a company's *success formula*. A founder's success formula can attract required funding, energize the team, and differentiate the organization from the competition.

Bold actions can enable outsized success. Success, in turn, can reassure managers that they have hit upon the one best way to compete. Of course, managers continue to make commitments—they invest capital, make public promises, and sign contracts. These actions, however, tend to reinforce the established success formula, usually causing it to harden. Initial success also provides managers with the financial wherewithal to commit further resources without investor approval. Over time, a company's success formula can take on a life of its own, independent of any competitive usefulness. People keep doing more of what worked in the past without questioning the underlying logic.

All of this is fine as long as the competitive environment continues to reward the company for maintaining the status quo. But dramatic shifts in the environment—changes, for example, in regulation, consumer tastes, or technology—can significantly devalue a company's historical success formula. Managers generally see the changes coming—indeed, these shifts are usually hard to miss. They attempt to respond by continuing or even accelerating actions that reinforce the existing success formula. I use the term *active inertia* to describe the organization's tendency to respond to even the most disruptive shifts in the environment by accelerating actions that worked in the past.

Companies trapped in active inertia can exhibit some strange behavior. They engage expensive consulting firms but fail to implement their recommendations. They adopt new technologies or business models without abandoning the old. They take a series of half steps that are too small to fix the fundamental problems but large enough to exhaust the management team and convince them they are doing something. The situation resembles a car with its back wheels stuck in a rut. Managers step on the gas, only to dig the hole deeper.

Many management academics have weighed all the factors reinforcing corporate inertia and concluded that changing a company's core business is, for all intents and purposes, impossible. A few influential streams of academic theory—including population ecology and evolutionary economics—draw their inspiration from evolutionary theory in biology.[1] These theories liken companies to living organisms. At birth, a company is imprinted with a set of characteristics analogous to an organism's genes. These characteristics endure over time and are difficult or impossible to alter. When a company's competitive environment changes, according to these evolutionary theories, the organization cannot adapt quickly enough to seize new opportunities or respond to threats. As a result, firms with a fixed genetic code die out like dinosaurs. Change, according to these theories, does not occur *within* an existing organization. Rather, the population of companies shifts as old companies exit and new ones take their place. The fittest survive until the environment shifts; then they too become extinct. No exceptions.

Influential books written for managers have followed a similar tack. According to one view, managers should respond to disruptive changes by creating a separate business unit because changing the core is too difficult and costly.[2] Other authors have argued that managers should simply accept the decline of successful companies as an inevitable, salutary feature of capitalism.[3] The recent failure of transformational efforts at high-profile companies such as Enron, Arthur Andersen, Vivendi, and AT&T seems to support this view.

Although evolutionary models can help us understand much of what goes on in a capitalist economy, they fail to account for the companies that *do* successfully adapt to changes in their competitive environment and *do* outlive their peer group. Some of these exceptions are well known: IBM, Nokia, and General Electric. Others are less familiar: Oticon, Samsung, Lloyds TSB, and Asahi Breweries. Evolutionary theorists might reply that these companies are rare exceptions. I agree. But these exceptions raise a critical question: If some companies can change their genetic code, then what prevents others from doing the same?

At the opposite extreme from evolutionary models, some leading management thinkers have argued for incessant *revolutionary*
change.[4] According to this view, managers can and should blow
up their existing success formula and rebuild it from scratch on a
regular basis. The revolutionary approach has two major limitations, in my opinion. First, by trying to change everything all at
once, managers often destroy crucial competencies embedded in
well-honed processes. Radical changes can also tear the fabric of
relationships that took years to weave, thereby disorienting customers, partners, and employees alike. Revolution undoubtedly
provides a jolt to the system, but the shock can prove fatal. The
metaphor of revolution also provides managers with little guidance on prioritizing or sequencing their actions. Changing everything all at once, in other words, is a recipe for chaos. While the
rhetoric of revolution may excite employees, customers, and
investors in the short term, its realities can destroy the company in
the long run. Presumably, how-to books entitled *Management
Lessons from the Cultural Revolution* or *Corporate Change the
Pol Pot Way* would find few readers.

My research suggests a third way between the extremes of
evolution and revolution. Managers can fundamentally change
their existing success formula. I introduce the phrase *transforming commitments* to describe managerial actions that break from
the status quo by increasing the cost of persisting in past behaviors or eliminating the possibility of doing so. Transforming commitments have little in common with the day-to-day actions—
such as budget approval or customer guarantees—that occupy
much of a manager's time. Rather, they resemble the founder's
commitments that define an organization's character in its formative years. Both mark a break from the past. Both require boldness, prudence, and tenacity.

When they make the commitments necessary for success,
however, managers set in motion an inescapable process of hardening that renders change more difficult when circumstances
change. The more successful its commitments, the harder a company will cling to them and the farther it will fall. The risk of get-

ting trapped by an obsolete success formula is particularly acute in dynamic competitive environments. Commitments, in short, have a shelf life. The notion of transforming commitments, however, offers the promise that past commitments are not destiny, and extinction is not inevitable. Revival of the fittest is possible, and managers can make the difference.

Hundreds of books have been written on corporate change. What could possibly be left for me to say? Simply this: *Bold commitments are a double-edged sword.* They enable outsized success but also constrain response when conditions change. Managers who understand the dual nature of commitments can wield them more effectively. Managers who don't will likely hurt themselves and their organizations by taking imprudent actions, persisting in the status quo for too long, or attempting to change without understanding the implications of their acts. This book serves as a user's guide for making, managing, and remaking commitments effectively. See box I-1 for a discussion of the genesis of and research for this book.

Who Should Read This Book

This book is written primarily for business leaders who face major changes in their environment and are struggling to respond effectively. My research included small companies as well as large firms, both high-technology and low-technology private and public companies drawn from a wide variety of industries and regions. As a result, the lessons in this book apply to a broad range of managers around the world. Managers in the social enterprise sector, including churches, charities, government agencies, and educational institutions, may also find these ideas and tools helpful in transforming their organizations in response to environmental changes. Like leading companies, many nonbusiness institutions require transformation: Consider the public schools in many American cities, the U.S. military as it wages a new kind of war on terrorism, or the Catholic church in the wake of the clergy

BOX I-1

How I Studied Commitments

MY INTEREST IN MANAGERIAL commitments and inertia is more than academic. As a young man growing up in Ohio, I observed a series of industry leaders—including U.S. Steel, General Motors, and Westinghouse—suffer prolonged and painful declines. As a consultant with McKinsey & Company and later a manager in a leveraged buyout, I worked firsthand with companies struggling to adapt to changes in their competitive environment.

My active research began a decade ago, when I entered the doctoral program at Harvard Business School and had the opportunity to systematically study why companies fail to respond effectively to changes in their context. I conducted an in-depth historical analysis of the U.S. tire industry's response to the radial tire technology introduced by Michelin in the 1970s. This research provided my first insight into how managers' historical commitments could influence their responses to environmental changes. The tire industry also provided an intriguing paradox. Firestone and Goodyear—two companies nearly identical in age, location, strategy, and organization—both faced new technology. Both initially responded with active inertia, yet Goodyear broke out of the rut while Firestone could not.

To test whether management commitments played a role in other companies' responses to environmental changes, I analyzed five additional pairs of companies. For each pair, I selected two companies that resembled one another closely in terms of strategy, size, location, and founding date. Each pair faced a major shift in its regulatory environment, consumer preferences, or technology. One company responded effectively and the other did not. (Successful response was measured by revenue growth, market share, and value created for shareholders.) The pairs were selected to provide diversity of regions, with two pairs each from North America,

Europe, and Asia. The pairs also varied in industry and the nature of the environmental change. The pairs also varied in industry and the nature of the environmental change. The pairs are summarized in table I-1. For each company, I collected data from company annual reports, published financial data, newspapers, industry trade journals, published case studies, books, and equity analysts' reports; created a database of key events; and coded the events using categories from my research. I also conducted more than one hundred interviews with current and former executives in these companies to supplement the published data.[5] In addition, I studied a series of unpaired companies—some successful, some not— in a variety of industries and regions, including Eastern Europe and South America.

Processing such voluminous case data was a nontrivial task, and I employed several approaches to analyze the data. I used the case studies to develop an M.B.A. course on managerial commitments and overcoming inertia at the London Business School. Our discussions enriched my understanding of the cases, and lectures provided an opportunity to present and discuss the emerging insights with a group of outstanding students. I also published a series of articles on commitments and inertia for scholars and managers, who provided valuable feedback that sharpened my thinking. To road-test my ideas in the real world, I worked with managers—in a wide range of industries and regions—who were struggling to transform their own organizations. These interactions helped translate concepts and theories into hands-on tools and exercises that managers could use to solve real problems. Many of these tools are included in this book.

I also submitted my ideas to the test of theory. By theory, I mean a simplified mental model of how something works in the real world.[6] A theory focuses attention on critical variables and describes how those variables influence each other. One prominent theory in economics, for example, models firms as black boxes that produce the level of output—think steel or cement—which maximizes profits at a given price. In the real world, of course, managers worry about factors in addition to profits—customer satisfaction, say, or public relations. They also make decisions about issues other than how much volume to produce. The power of theory does not lie in describing reality in all its richness and complexity. That is the job of Russian novelists. Rather, good theory provides a kind of x-ray vision that focuses attention on the critical issues for action. There is nothing more useful, it turns out, than a good theory.

The field of management draws on three primary disciplines—economics, sociology, and psychology. Outstanding scholars in each of these fields have thought long and hard about commitments. Over the past ten years, I have spent countless hours reading and digesting these works. The findings from their inquiries helped me to tighten and refine my own thinking about managerial commitments. In addition to these core disciplines, I read selectively in other fields, including history, rhetoric, poetry, linguistics, and evolutionary biology, to understand how scholars in those traditions have thought about commitments. I have summarized some of the more interesting insights from these forays into other fields in sidebars throughout this book.

sexual abuse scandal, to name just a few prominent examples. I hope that leaders in a wide array of organizations will benefit from this book.

"Great," you may be saying to yourself, "but I'm far too busy to read a book." But *that* may be exactly the problem. When people are trapped in active inertia, they often exhaust themselves with relentless activity—fighting fires and responding to immediate crises—without ever pausing to step back and ask whether all

TABLE I-1

Summary of Matched Pairs in Research Sample

Industry	Change in Environment	Time Period	Region	Successful	Less Successful
Tires	Radial tire technology	1970s	U.S.	Goodyear	Firestone
Telecommunications equipment	Mobile telephony	1990s	Scandanavia	Nokia	Ericsson
Personal computers	Low-cost clones	1990s	U.S.	Compaq	Apple
Conglomerates	Decreased government support	1990s	South Korea	Samsung	Daewoo
Consumer banking	"Big bang" deregulation	1980s	U.K.	Lloyds TSB	National Westminster
Brewing	Shift in consumer tastes	1980s	Japan	Asahi	Sapporo

their frenzied activity is accomplishing anything useful. They dig frantically to escape the hole, but only dig themselves in deeper.

This book provides managers an opportunity to step out of their day-to-day activity, assess whether their organization is trapped by its past commitments, and develop a concrete plan of action to pull it from its rut. Each chapter contains real-life examples. Throughout the book, I have included exercises, diagnostic tests, hands-on tools, common mistakes to avoid, helpful questions, and little tips—all drawn from research, informed by theory, and, more important, field-tested in the real world with real managers. The book is organized as follows:

- *Chapter 1: The Life Cycle of Commitments.* The first chapter introduces managerial commitments as a powerful lens through which to understand how companies succeed in the first place, become trapped by their past, and can be transformed by managers when the environment shifts.

- *Chapter 2: The Active Inertia Trap.* This chapter uses case studies from a variety of industries and regions to illustrate how a company's success formula can harden and lead to a pathological inability to adapt.

- *Chapter 3: Is Your Company at Risk?* This chapter presents a set of hands-on diagnostics that managers can use to assess whether their own organization is suffering from active inertia.

- *Chapter 4: The Power of Transforming Commitments.* This chapter helps managers assess whether transforming commitments are right for their own company and describes a three-step process they can follow to transform their organization.

- *Chapter 5: Choosing the Right Anchor.* Managers can commit to new strategic frames, processes, resources, relationships, or values to transform their organization. This chapter reviews their respective pros and cons.

- *Chapter 6: Picking the Right Person for the Job.* The success of transforming commitments depends to a large extent on who makes them. This chapter provides insights on how to select the right managers and enable them to get the job done.

- *Chapter 7: Giving Your Commitments Traction.* Managers' commitments to change are often dismissed as cheap talk that is too fuzzy or too little, too late. This chapter introduces the "three Cs" of effective commitments—credible, clear, and courageous—that managers can use to strengthen their commitments.

- *Chapter 8: The Seven Deadly Sins of Transforming Commitments.* This chapter lists seven common mistakes that can derail transformation efforts and illustrates them with examples from recent failed transformations, including Arthur Andersen, AT&T, Bertelsmann, Compaq, Enron, Kmart, Sunbeam, and Vivendi, among others.

- *Chapter 9: The Private Side of Public Commitments.* Transforming commitments have personal costs and benefits. This chapter helps managers weigh the personal trade-offs before committing to transformation.

Revival
of the
Fittest

ONE

The Life Cycle of Commitments

WHAT DO MANAGERS REALLY DO? Many people equate the manager's job with strategy—deciding where and how an organization will compete. Another group of scholars says that executives primarily develop and manage processes, including operations, decision making, and resource allocation. Others argue that a manager should, above all, nurture a distinctive culture.

These familiar views of management are all valid, but in this chapter, I introduce a fresh perspective: Managers select, make, honor, and sometimes remake commitments. These commitments can be bet-the-company decisions, such as investing in a new technology or exiting a business, or they can be routine actions, such as guaranteeing customer quality or promising to achieve a budget target. These commitments have one feature in common: They bind the organization to a specified behavior in the future.

Studying managerial commitments can help us understand how companies initially succeed, may subsequently get locked

BOX 1-1

Alternative Perspectives on Commitments

ECONOMISTS, SOCIOLOGISTS, and psychologists use the term *commitment* in very different ways. So how does my construct of managerial commitments differ from these other definitions? First, note that in my terminology commitments are *actions*, not a person's state of attachment to, say, an organization or its goals.[1] The term commitment sometimes describes the persistence of an organization's strategy or an individual's behavior over time, but again, that is not what I mean.[2]

Also note that my definition links two levels—the manager and the organization—whereas much of the academic literature on commitment has focused exclusively on the individual. Scholars have examined, for example, how individuals act in the present to lock themselves into a desired behavior in the future.[3] A common example is publicly pledging to quit smoking to increase the future cost (lost reputation, ribbing from friends) that would be incurred

---

into inertia, and ultimately adapt (or fail to adapt) to changes in their environment. This chapter defines managerial commitments, lists various mechanisms that managers use to commit, reviews the benefits and costs of commitments, and examines how commitments evolve over time.

What Are Managerial Commitments?

Managerial commitments are the cornerstone of my model. I define *managerial commitments* as any actions that an entrepreneur or manager takes that bind the organization to specific

by lighting up again. This commitment binds only the individual who made it, not a larger organization.

Other scholars analyze commitments without accounting for people. Economists in the field of industrial organization, for example, simply assume that they can model a firm as a "black box" that maximizes value. These models explore how a firm's commitments, such as capacity expansion or advertising, affect competition.[4] These models provide insights into competitive dynamics, but fail to account for the role of individuals in managing commitments. The specific person who undertakes the commitments matters a great deal, as I will argue in subsequent chapters.

One prominent stream of thinking *has* explored commitments across the individual and organizational levels of analysis. This body of research—known as "escalating commitment to a failed course of action"—examines how a manager's public statements can diminish the manager's ability or willingness to kill a money-losing project. As the name suggests, however, this work focuses on the pathological aspects of commitments and offers little insight on their benefits.[5]

behaviors in the future.[6] (Box 1-1 explains how this definition of commitment relates to different uses of the term in scholarly literature.) Managers commit their organizations to future actions all the time, sometimes without even recognizing that they have done so. The following list, though by no means a mutually exclusive or exhaustive taxonomy of commitments, describes the most common binding actions that I have observed in my research.[7]

- *Invest capital.* Managers can commit their organization to a course of action by investing cash to support that course. All investment involves betting some money in the present—for research and development, acquisitions, or advertising, for instance—to earn more in the future. Managers can also invest by sacrificing current profits. When Intel launched the Pentium chip, for example, the company cannibalized sales of its existing microprocessors. These forgone profits were an investment that committed the company to the new chip's success.

- *Make personnel decisions.* Managers also allocate human capital—for example, by hiring more employees to staff a new initiative, moving seasoned executives from a profitable division to a new venture, or firing managers who undermine the new direction. People decisions are powerful mechanisms for committing an organization to a course of action.

- *Exit.* Managers can commit by closing off options—for example, by reducing capacity in an ongoing business or by exiting a business altogether through sale or closure.[8] Exit decisions bind a company most effectively when restarting or reacquiring the operations would take too much money or time. If Ford could quickly and cheaply restart a factory, for example, or buy capacity on the market, then its plant closures would not be very binding.

- *Make public promises.* Managers can bind an organization by publicly pledging that the company will do something. Recall Michael Armstrong's promise that AT&T would achieve millions of cable-based telephone subscribers. The act of pledging publicly creates costs that the manager and company will incur by failing to deliver on the promise. For example, the company's reputation may suffer, making it harder to persuade customers to buy, shareholders to invest, or competitors to stay out.[9] The individual manager also puts his personal reputation on the line, and he will likely do whatever he can to honor the pledge and avoid the psychological cost of admitting his miscalculation.[10]

- *Make public assertions.* Managers can also bind their organization by publicly declaring something to be true.[11] For example, a founder might assert that a specific rival poses the most danger, a specific group of customers matters the most, or that a single technology poses the greatest threat. By committing to the truth of these statements, the manager implies that she will act as if these statements were true. Expecting as much, employees, partners, and customers may modify their behavior accordingly. Managers often stick to their assertions to avoid the embarrassment of admitting they were wrong.

- *Forge relationships with resource providers.* Managers often make decisions that satisfy the requirements of external stakeholders—such as banks or customers—that provide necessary resources but may not be in the firm's best interests.[12] Public companies, for example, must respond to the demands of investors. Recent research suggests that firms meet the demands of their biggest customers, even when this response might harm these firms in the long term.[13] Customers and investors constitute the obvious relationships, but companies may also depend on partnerships with firms that provide complementary products. The fates of Intel and Microsoft, for example, were tightly intertwined for years. Belonging to groups—such as standards-setting organizations or industry associations—can also limit companies' discretion.[14]

  These relationships do not arise out of thin air, however, but result from earlier actions that led the company to depend on investors, customers, or partners for money, technology, or complementary products in the first place. Lucent, for example, may have been a "slave to Wall Street" as some business commentators have argued.[15] However, its position resulted from managers' choice to spin off the business as a public company. Of course, no company can avoid entering into dependent relationships altogether. Entrepreneurs and managers can, however, exercise discretion when initiating these relationships.

- *Write an explicit contract.* Contracts also bind organizations to a course of action. Like a public promise, an explicit contract puts managerial and corporate reputations at stake. The reputational damage from breaching a contract can persuade managers to honor a contract—even when it does not spell out every possible contingency and required response.[16] In addition, explicit contracts often limit a manager's discretion by transferring responsibility for monitoring and enforcing the contract to a third party, such as a court or an arbitration body.
- *Manipulate information.* Managers can focus employees through their selection of metrics and control systems.[17] What gets measured, as the old saying goes, gets done. Managers can strengthen this commitment by linking incentives to the metrics.[18] Employees whose bonuses depend on the success of a new venture, for example, are more motivated to ensure success than those whose compensation depends on how long they've been with the company.

Commitments as Double-Edged Swords

Managers sometimes commit unwittingly or unconsciously. Often, however, they use commitments deliberately as a means to an end. Commitments can provide a sustainable advantage relative to competitors. Replicating investments in technology or brand building, for example, can prove difficult and thereby prevent competitors from rapidly copying what the firm does.[19] Commitments can also influence competitors' behavior.[20] Large investments in fixed capacity, for example, can deter potential competitors from entering a market.

Commitments can also persuade other firms to produce complementary products.[21] IBM's big investment in personal computers in the early 1980s, for example, convinced independent software vendors to write code for IBM's machine. Commitments can also persuade consumers to adopt a new technology (remember that nobody ever got fired for buying an IBM) or to side with one technology when two conflicting platforms are engaged in a "standards war"—think Wintel versus Mac.[22]

In addition to their competitive advantages, commitments also provide organizational benefits. Public statements of a clear strategy, for example, can focus employees' attention and help them coordinate their activities. A pledge to achieve a goal backed up with action can create and mobilize energy among employees and induce employees to persist even the outcome is far from certain.[23]

The act of committing to a desired future state can, under the right circumstances, increase the probability that the desired future will come to pass—creating, in effect, a self-fulfilling prophecy.[24] Bold commitments can deter competitors, build valuable resources, induce cooperation from partners, convince customers to join, and energize employees. Of course, these benefits do not guarantee success. Rather, when the action is right for the situation, then bold commitments can fuel a self-fulfilling prophecy that increases the likelihood of success.

Managers commit to reap these competitive and organizational benefits. Commitments come at a cost, however: They limit an organization's flexibility in the present. By focusing on one way of developing new products, for example, a company may excel at innovation in one domain but become less competent in other technologies.[25] Commitments may lock an organization into pathological persistence in a course of action, despite negative feedback.[26] Managers' commitments can also limit an organization's ability to adapt to unpredictable changes in its environment.[27] Early commitments may have unintended consequences that impair the organization in unforeseen ways, or the external environment might shift in an unanticipated way that renders the organization's former strengths into liabilities.

The Life Cycle of Commitments

People often refer to companies as passing through stages in a life cycle: After their birth as start-ups, firms enter a gangly adolescence, mature, and ultimately decline and die.[28] Although this analogy to a biological life cycle appears plausible at first glance, it fails to account for companies, such as Nokia or IBM, that have reversed the flow of time and recaptured the vibrancy of their youth. A framework of managerial commitments provides a theoretical lens for understanding not only why companies pass through predictable stages, but also how some repeatedly tap the fountain of youth.

I use the phrase *life cycle of commitments* to describe my framework. The story is simple: In a company's early years, founders and other managers make a series of commitments—to a strategy, a set of processes, resources, values, and relationships with investors, customers, and partners. These early actions—which I call *defining commitments*—form the essential character of the organization going forward.[29] As the organization matures, managers continue to make investments, promises, public statements, and personnel decisions and to take other actions that bind their company. Historical commitments—embodied in the existing organization—however, tend to constrain their actions. As a result, managers' subsequent commitments often reinforce the existing organization—hence the name *reinforcing commitments*.[30]

Reinforcing commitments serve a company well as long as the organization aligns with its external environment. When the external environment shifts, however, a gap can grow between the environment and the organization. At this point, managers must make *transforming commitments* that fundamentally realign the organization with the new environmental conditions.

So, with this model, where does the rubber meet the road? The remainder of this section explores the life cycle of commitments model through the tire industry—specifically, the history of Firestone and Goodyear.

Defining Commitments

During the first three decades of the twentieth century, the tire was the semiconductor of its day, and the tire sector was a hotbed of technical innovation.[31] (See figure 1-1.) Tire makers provided a critical component to automobile manufacturers, then the fastest-growing industry in the world, and erected some of the earliest dedicated research labs in the country, trailing only the chemical industry in research intensity. The research led to dramatic improvements: In 1900, the average tire lasted five hundred miles and was unsafe at any speed; in the next thirty-five years, the typical tire's useful life increased fortyfold while prices dropped 80 percent.

Explosive growth, technical ferment, and low barriers to entry attracted hundreds of entrepreneurs to the industry, concentrated in Akron, Ohio. Between 1900 and 1923, more than five hundred start-ups entered the tire industry, and by 1926 Akron-based firms produced approximately 60 percent of tires made in the United States. While no one would confuse Akron's climate with Silicon Valley's, the city was an epicenter of entrepreneurial

FIGURE 1-1

Akron: The Silicon Valley of the Early 1900s

- Sales of automobiles increased a thousandfold between 1900 and 1923.
- Passenger tire shipments grew from 2 million in 1910 to 59 million in 1925.
- More than 500 companies entered the tire industry between 1900 and 1934.
- By 1920, the tire industry had produced 122 millionaires in Akron alone.
- The average life of a tire increased from 500 miles in 1900 to 20,000 miles by 1923.
- The average price of a tire fell 80 percent in 25 years.
- The tire industry was the second most research-intensive industry in the United States in the 1920s (chemicals was first).
- Tire makers were among the first American firms to establish dedicated research labs.
- The tire industry enjoyed the second-highest rate of labor productivity increases between 1914 and 1934, as tires per man-hour increased from 30 to 160.
- By 1926, 60 percent of all American tire production took place in Akron.
- Between 1910 and 1920, Akron was the fastest-growing city in the United States.

Source: Donald N. Sull, "From Community of Innovation to Community of Inertia: The Rise and Fall of the Akron Tire Cluster," in *The Academy of Management Best Paper Proceedings* (Washington, DC: Academy of Management, 2001).

wealth creation. In 1920, two Akron journalists estimated that the city's tire industry had minted 122 millionaires.

In 1900, Harvey S. Firestone moved to Akron and founded the Firestone Tire & Rubber Company. In his company's formative years, Firestone made a series of defining commitments that determined the nature of his company. Firestone—like other founders and early managers—did not make these commitments all at once, but staged them over time.[32] To keep their options open, entrepreneurs generally avoid binding commitments for as long as possible until they absolutely must act to get the resources necessary for pursuing an opportunity. Common examples of defining commitments include serving a single customer or market segment, investing in only one technology, or going public to raise additional capital. Founders or early managers often make these commitments without recognizing that their decisions will shape the organization going forward. Defining commitments fall into five broad categories: strategic frames, resources, processes, relationships, and values.

- *Strategic frames.* These are the shared mental models that shape how managers and employees view the world.[33] Shared strategic frames allow employees and managers to provide the same answers to key strategic questions: What business are we in? Who are our most dangerous competitors? Who are our most important allies? How do we create value? What must we do in-house? Which customers are critical to success? Which can we safely ignore?

  Shared strategic frames can prevent growing companies from spinning off in a hundred different directions. Harvey Firestone, for example, defined his opportunity as rubber tires. This framing seems obvious now, but in 1900, only a few thousand automobiles were produced, and the country lacked a reliable road system. Automobiles were a rich person's toy, like a private jet today. Firestone's framing of the opportunity—implicit in the

company's name, Firestone Tire & Rubber—focused
employees on rubber tires and enabled them to react
quickly when demand for automobiles, and thus tires,
exploded. Established companies such as U.S. Rubber that
defined themselves as rubber companies producing items
like raingear, syringes, and fire hoses lost tire market share
to focused players such as Firestone and Goodyear.

- *Resources.* Managers also commit to resources. Broadly
  speaking, resources can include tangible assets, such as
  land, plants, and equipment, as well as intangible ones,
  such as brands, patents, and technology.[34] Note that not
  every resource investment locks a firm into a course of
  action. A manager could, for example, purchase shares of
  another corporation in the public equity markets and sell
  them the next day. A resource must have three characteristics to constitute a defining commitment.[35] First, the
  resources must be *durable* and thus capable of exerting
  influence in the future. Resources must also be *specialized*,
  which means they cannot be deployed easily to different
  strategies and therefore lock the firm into a future
  behavior. Finally, resources must be *illiquid*, or difficult
  to buy and sell in factor markets. Otherwise, managers
  could easily sell the resources and use the cash to buy
  other resources for pursuing an alternative direction.[36]

What type of investment in a resource locks a firm into
a future course of action? Advertising to build a brand is a
good example. Harvey Firestone, a pioneer in sports marketing, invested heavily in the company's brand, and he
sponsored the winner of the inaugural Indianapolis 500.
The resulting brand was durable; it would have persisted
even without more advertising. It was also specialized.
Firestone could not have easily extended the brand to a
radically different product like a soft drink, clearly outside
Firestone's expertise. Finally, the brand would be difficult

(although not impossible) to buy, sell, or license, partly because of its specialized meaning.

Firestone also invested in other resources that were durable, specialized, and illiquid. The company initially outsourced manufacturing and focused on marketing. In 1902, Harvey Firestone decided to bring production in-house and built a tire factory in Akron. The company subsequently invested heavily in manufacturing capacity and in R&D; and the resulting assets—the sprawling factory complex and product technology—were both specialized and durable. Firestone's product innovations included a novel rim and clincher that attached the tire to the wheel. This innovation allowed Firestone to bypass a competitor's patent on tire design that had effectively barred Firestone from a large share of the market.

- *Processes.* Processes, as I use the term, refers to how things get done in an organization and includes both formal and informal procedures.[37] The term encompasses a broad range of recurrent processes within an organization, including production, logistics, decision making, hiring and training, new product development, and investment. Committing to specific processes frees people to focus on value-creating tasks and confers productivity gains as employees move up the experience curve.[38] Agreed-upon processes also coordinate the activities of a complex organization across the company's boundaries. This predictability of behavior brings legitimacy, which increases a new firm's odds of survival.[39]

In Firestone's formative years, its managers focused on improving manufacturing. After several years of experimentation and incremental improvements, they perfected the process of "gum-dipping" in which strips of cloth were completely permeated with rubber and then cured to assume a uniform shape. Gum-dipping enabled Firestone to improve tire life, ride, and safety substantially, thereby enhancing its competitive position. Firestone heavily advertised the gum-dipped manufacturing process to differentiate the product and installed the procedure in all new tire plants.

- *Relationships.* Entrepreneurs also commit to a set of relationships with external individuals and organizations—customers, shareholders, suppliers, and regulators—that provide needed resources, including such intangibles as managerial insight, scrupulous reputation, and legitimacy. Early relationships with high-status organizations can enable the new venture to attract other quality resources more easily.[40] Entrepreneurs solidify these relationships through several mechanisms, including investing to serve customers' needs, learning to work with a specific supplier, or building trust with partners.[41] In some cases, managers deepen business associations with personal friendships and blood relations. Interweaving the warp of economic transactions with the woof of social relationships can strengthen a company's fabric so that it can withstand the toughest of competitive climates. Entrepreneurs also commit to relationships within the firm. They decide which activities to outsource, which to do in-house, and how to organize the internal business units.[42]

Harvey Firestone committed to key customers. While working for his uncle in Detroit, Firestone met a struggling entrepreneur named Henry Ford. Firestone kept in touch after moving to Akron and made his first sale to Ford in 1906. The company continued to supply approximately one-half of Ford's tires, which represented a serious volume once the Model T was launched in 1908. Firestone solidified his relationship with Ford by organizing and underwriting several camping trips in which the two men enjoyed the company of Thomas Edison, naturalist John Burroughs, and two U.S. presidents, among others. Although these excursions hardly qualified as roughing it—the entourage included a full-sized player piano, six thoroughbred horses, and a small army of servants—they did allow Firestone to secure his ties with Ford.

- *Values.* Managers often commit to a strong set of values, or shared norms, that unite and inspire organizational participants.[43] Strong values can spark employee loyalty and strengthen the bonds with customers who appreciate the firm's ideology. These corporate values can be traditional—like Laura Ashley's modest virtue or Walt Disney's family fun—or cutting edge, as with Prada's changeability or Crunch gyms. Regardless of content, companies with strong values can attract like-minded consumers and employees. Harvey Firestone committed to a set of corporate values to bind his company "as a family." In an era of widespread labor strife, Firestone viewed his workers paternalistically. In 1916, he drew on Firestone Tire corporate coffers to construct Firestone Park, a one-thousand-unit residential community providing low-cost homes for employees. In that same year, he introduced an eight-hour workday for all employees.

Defining commitments can confer benefits that outweigh their costs in terms of forgone flexibility, as was the case for Firestone. As Ford rose to industry dominance, the company pulled its major suppliers—including Firestone—along for the ride. Firestone's investment in product and process technology kept the firm at the cutting edge of a rapidly evolving technology, well ahead of the many start-ups in the tire industry.[44] Firestone's commitments to "family values" attracted and retained scarce technical and production talent in Akron's overheated labor market.

Harvey Firestone's commitments paid handsome dividends as the tire industry's boom went bust during the 1920s. By the middle of the decade, the number of new entrepreneurs had slowed to a trickle, while firms exiting grew to a flood. (See figure 1-2.) The total number of manufacturers declined from a peak of 274 in 1922 to just over 50 by 1937. By 1935, Firestone had emerged

FIGURE 1-2

Exit and Entry of U.S. Tire Firms: 1914–1937

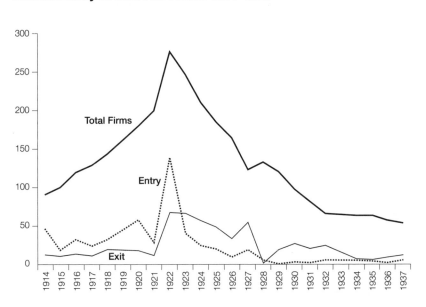

Source: Donald N. Sull, "From Community of Innovation to Community of Inertia: The Rise and Fall of the Akron Tire Cluster," working paper 01-025, Harvard Business School, Boston, 2001, table 2. Data interpolated for 1919 and 1933.

from the shakeout as the third-largest U.S. tire firm and the sixti-eth-largest industrial enterprise in the United States.

Reinforcing Commitments

Managers continue to make commitments beyond a com-pany's formative years, of course. Their new commitments no longer define the organization. Rather, they tend to reinforce the existing organization, which has begun to shape management's thinking. Typical examples of reinforcing commitments include budget agreements, job assignments, customer guarantees, and investments that occupy much of a manager's day-to-day routine in an established enterprise. Reinforcing commitments can consist of major actions—large investments or bold public promises—or a series of small steps that build on the past. After a while, they resemble the ruts cut by the wheels of many carts along a dirt path. The established grooves channel the cart's path, and each passing vehicle deepens the rut.

Managers make reinforcing commitments for good reasons. Initial investments in R&D, for example, decrease the risks and costs of investing in related technology. Building on partner-specific trust and knowledge is easier than forging new relationships from scratch. It is generally less expensive to retain established customers than acquire new ones. The same logic holds for employees. Refining an existing strategic frame is less problematic than completely rethinking the company's business—reinventing the wheel, so to speak. Extending processes is less disruptive than reengineering them.

After Harvey Firestone died in 1938, his successors made a steady series of commitments that reinforced his legacy. The company integrated backward into components and raw materials— including a million-acre rubber plantation in Liberia. His successors also integrated forward into dedicated retail tire stores, built new factories that replicated the company's existing manufacturing process, and hired and promoted new managers steeped in the company's values. In the early 1970s, all of Firestone's top managers had spent their entire career with the company, two-thirds were Akron born and bred, and one-third followed in their fathers' footsteps as Firestone executives. Such managers were called "gum dipped." The ties binding the Firestone and Ford companies were knotted tighter when Harvey Firestone's granddaughter married William Clay Ford, then the largest Ford shareholder.

Had the ghost of Harvey Firestone returned to Akron in the late 1960s, he would have found that remarkably little had changed since his death. As other companies acquired unrelated businesses during the takeover wave of the 1960s, Harvey Firestone's company had remained unfashionably faithful to its core tire business, diversifying only into closely related businesses like steel wheels. Tires still employed the basic design developed during Firestone's lifetime, still lasted approximately twenty thousand miles, and were still manufactured using essentially the same decades-old process. Ford remained the company's largest customer.

Continuity of a company's success formula can confer efficiency and focus that help a company compete in a stable environment. However, when the competitive context shifts, a company's strengths can become weaknesses and its assets, liabilities. This happened to Firestone when Michelin introduced the radial tire into the U.S. market. Michelin's radial tire was superior to the traditional technology (known as bias tires) on almost every dimension that mattered to consumers. The radial lasted twice as long, reduced the chances of a catastrophic failure or "blowout," and improved fuel economy an average of 5 percent to 10 percent.

When François Michelin assumed control of the family firm in 1955, he decided to leverage Michelin's lead in radial technology to industry dominance. During the 1960s, Michelin aggressively expanded its radial production capacity in Europe and thereby increased European radial penetration from under 10 percent to nearly 75 percent. Michelin's successful assault triggered a massive exit and consolidation among incumbent tire makers in Germany, Austria, England, and Italy. By the early 1970s, Michelin had emerged as the undisputed leader in the European tire industry.

Firestone had ringside seats to watch Michelin pummel its European competitors. Firestone had competed in Europe for decades and was among the top ten tire producers there. The action moved closer to home in the mid-1960s, when Michelin began producing radial tires for Sears, announced its plans to build a North American factory, and placed radial tires on the Lincoln Continental.

Firestone managers saw radials coming. Indeed, radials were impossible to miss. They responded quickly and aggressively. The managers' response, however, was channeled by their existing strategic frames, resources, processes, relationships, and values. Firestone, along with the other U.S. tire companies, reacted to the radial tire by introducing an incremental extension of its existing tire design and then trumpeting this as an alternative to radials.

This extension (known as belted-bias) initially gained market share based on aggressive advertising that promised outstanding performance. Sales of the new design deflated, however, as consumers realized that they were essentially no different from the old tires. (See figure 1-3 for the market share of tire types.)

Akron's belted-bias initiative failed to dull Detroit's growing interest in radial tires. In 1972, Ford announced its intention to place radials on all models over the following few years. General Motors quickly followed suit. Firestone managers rapidly responded to Ford's request and decided to build a new factory dedicated to radial production. They also invested to convert existing capacity to radial production. Firestone managers decided to manufacture radials using their existing manufacturing process with minor modifications. The decision to leverage existing manufacturing processes allowed Firestone to ramp up volume quickly, but may have contributed to quality problems with the company's tires. In 1978, Firestone agreed to a voluntary recall

FIGURE 1-3

Market Share of Tire Types: 1961–1988

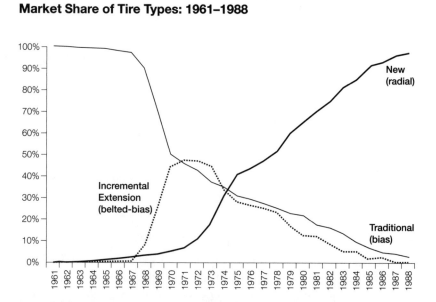

Source: Donald N. Sull, "The Dynamics of Standing Still: Firestone Tire & Rubber and the Radial Revolution," *Business History Review* 73, no. 3 (1999): 430–464.

of 8.7 million Firestone 500 tires at a cost of $150 million after taxes—an action that constituted the largest consumer recall in U.S. history to that time.[45]

Although Firestone managers invested in radial tire capacity, they failed to close the bias tire plants rendered obsolete by that investment. The arithmetic of radials was simple. Radial tires lasted twice as long as the traditional tires they replaced. Consumers, as a result, would buy replacement radial tires approximately half as often as in the past. This meant that the industry needed fewer plants. American tire makers were ultimately forced to close twenty-nine of the fifty-seven domestic plants operating when Michelin began its U.S. invasion. Firestone managers did not pull their weight in closing plants. Although the company controlled a 24 percent share of the market, managers closed only a single plant, even after they invested heavily in the new technology. The cost of keeping money-losing plants exceeded the expense of covering the Firestone 500 write-off.

Firestone's "family values" help explain these costly delays. Firestone executives resisted investor and board pressure to close plants largely to shield the affected employees and communities. In his addresses to shareholders, Firestone's CEO repeatedly referred to employees and communities as part of the "worldwide Firestone family" and requested investors' patience while management tried to increase profits without layoffs.

Shareholders' patience ultimately ran out. Over seven hundred irate investors crowded into the company's 1979 stockholders' meeting, in which dissident investors proposed firing top management, liquidating the company, and distributing the proceeds to owners. Within a year, an outsider replaced the "gum-dipped" CEO. The new broom swept the company clean and led a major restructuring that saved the company from bankruptcy. In 1988, Japanese tire maker Bridgestone ultimately acquired Firestone, but the merger did not end all of Firestone's problems. In 2000, the brand was embroiled in a highly publicized dispute with longtime partner Ford over tires placed on Ford Explorers. The following year, Bridgestone/Firestone executives terminated the relationship with Ford after nearly a century of supplying the company with tires.

Transforming Commitments

Goodyear Tire & Rubber Company provides an instructive contrast. Like Harvey Firestone, Goodyear's founders defined their opportunity as rubber tires. Both companies had their head-quarters in Akron. Goodyear's founders forged a close relation-ship with W. C. Durant, CEO of General Motors (GM) in Detroit, which made Goodyear tires the standard on GM vehicles for years to come. Goodyear managers also committed to a strongly paternalistic set of values. They built a two-thousand-unit hous-ing development for employees—Goodyear Heights—and pio-neered innovations in worker health, safety, recreation, and train-ing. These commitments paid off for Goodyear as they had for Firestone, and by 1916, Goodyear had emerged as the leading tire company in the United States.

Like their counterparts at Firestone, Goodyear managers made a series of commitments that reinforced their existing trajec-tory: They replicated their manufacturing processes in new plants, integrated backward into raw material production, integrated forward into dedicated retailing, and invested heavily in the Akron community. Entering the 1970s, Goodyear and Firestone looked very similar as number one and two in the market. Goodyear's top management team could also be characterized as "gum-dipped." Two-thirds of Goodyear's top managers had spent their entire career in the company, one-third (including the CEO) had been born and raised in Akron, and one-half had risen through the ranks of the domestic tire business.

Like Firestone, Goodyear managers initially stumbled in responding to radials. Goodyear took the lead in promoting the ill-fated belted-bias tire as an alternative to the radial tire. But here is where the similarity ends. In 1972, Charles Pilliod was appointed president. Pilliod had spent nearly his entire career in

Goodyear's International Division, including a three-year stint in England, where he witnessed Michelin's rout firsthand. Upon taking the helm, he committed to world leadership in radial tire technology.

Pilliod bulldozed through internal resistance. When Goodyear's research department failed to produce figures supporting a large investment in radial technology, the new CEO informed them they were wrong based on his experience in Europe and ordered them to review the numbers. Rather than rely on Goodyear's existing manufacturing processes, Pilliod created technical teams to scour the world for the best available process technology to license. Goodyear executives were also quicker to exit the old technology. Goodyear closed its first domestic tire plant in 1975, three years before Firestone, and closed the remaining plants before they became major financial drains. Consequently, the company successfully defended its leadership in the global tire industry.

Managerial commitments, to recap this chapter's central argument, have a life cycle. An entrepreneur's *defining commitments* to strategic frames, resources, processes, relationships, and values can contribute to an organization's initial success and shape the organization's character going forward. Subsequent commitments tend to reinforce and be shaped by the prevailing status quo. *Reinforcing commitments* can lock an organization into a set trajectory, and managers struggle to change when the environment shifts. The Goodyear story illustrates, however, that commitments are not destiny. Managers can make *transforming commitments* that allow their organization to adapt to shifts in the competitive environment.

TWO

The Active Inertia Trap

IT'S TEMPTING TO DISMISS Firestone's failure as an artifact of a bygone era. But in fact, the Firestone story illustrates a recurring dynamic in business history. It goes like this: A successful company faces dramatic changes in its environment. Top executives watch anxiously as sales and profits erode, talented people leave, and market capitalization plummets. Some of these companies—such as Goodyear—stumble and return to greatness. Many firms, like Firestone, never recover. They shuffle along as shadows of their former glory or as subsidiaries of rivals. Consider the computer industry: IBM's revival is the exception among one-time leaders, including Digital Equipment Corporation, Data General, and Wang Laboratories.

What Is Active Inertia?

Why do good companies go bad? Sometimes they falter in the wake of a sudden, unforeseen jolt, as the travel industry did after the terrorist attacks of September 2001.[1] Such unforeseeable shocks are like meteorites in biological evolution; they come out of the blue and can cause extinction. Despite our best prognostic tools, we cannot forecast these events.

Unexpected jolts are dramatic, but they are also comparatively rare, at least among the firms in my sample. The more common environmental shifts happen gradually, and managers can and usually do anticipate them. *So why do managers fail to respond effectively when they see these changes coming?* Are they paralyzed and witless, like deer caught in the headlights of an oncoming car? The short answer is no. This explanation doesn't fit the facts. In my study of dozens of falling stars, I found top managers to be:

- *Farsighted and methodical.* Top executives invariably anticipate the changes and often commission a series of expensive reports from management consultants to detail the competitive shifts.

- *Active and dedicated.* Managers in these companies often log more hours per week than their counterparts elsewhere who are coping more effectively.

- *Bright and accomplished.* These managers are the same executives who achieved the company's past success.

If good managers foresee change and respond promptly, why do their actions fail? Managers respond quickly, forcefully, and yet *ineffectively* for many reasons, ranging from managerial arrogance to insufficient resources. My research, however, suggests another cause. Managers get trapped by success, a condition that I call *active inertia,* or management's tendency to respond to the most disruptive changes by accelerating activities that succeeded in the past.[2] When the world changes, in other words, they respond with more of what worked before. Recall Firestone's response to radial tires: Managers extended their existing technology, made radial tires on existing equipment, and maintained superfluous factories. These actions had served Firestone well in the past but proved disastrous against all-new technology. Of course, changes can come from many directions besides technical innovation, such as shifts in regulation, consumer preferences, and competitive dynamics.

Managers often equate inertia with inaction—a passive phenomenon in which organizations change more slowly than their environment or fail to change altogether, like the deer in the headlights.[3] But that rarely happens. A better analogy is a car stuck in a rut: Managers put the pedal to the metal—and dig the rut deeper. The word "active" highlights the reality that market leaders rarely freeze up when faced with change; rather, they escalate tried-and-true methods that prove ineffective in a changed context. So what locks companies into active inertia? The rest of this chapter explores several possible reasons.

A Success Formula Hardens

Active inertia stems from a company's defining commitments, the very actions that enabled its initial success. Entrepreneurs may follow a grand design in making their defining commitments, or they may take binding actions to seize unexpected opportunities or respond to pressing problems. Either way, their bundle of defining commitments coalesces over time into what I call a company's *success formula*, the company's unique set of strategic frames, resources, processes, relationships, and values that collectively influence managers' subsequent actions. (See box 2-1 for a discussion of how a success formula builds on and extends other theories; figure 2-1.) A clear success formula confers many benefits. It allows employees to concentrate on their strengths and thereby increases efficiency. Focus prevents employees from dissipating energy on peripheral opportunities. Common processes and clear reporting lines allow a company to scale as revenues grow. In a crowded field, a distinctive formula can differentiate the company from its rivals.

BOX 2-1

Duality and the Life Cycle of Commitments

THE NOTION OF A success formula, and the life cycle of commitments model more generally, builds on a theory of structure developed by the English sociologist Anthony Giddens.[4] Giddens addresses a fundamental question in sociology: How can we reconcile the existence of enduring structures constraining our action with the fact that we ourselves create, reinforce, and sometimes change these institutions? Giddens introduces the construct of the duality of structure to resolve this question. In Giddens's theory, people create and reinforce enduring social structures through their actions. These structures, in turn, constrain their subsequent actions. Duality emphasizes that structure is a coin with two sides. A structure results from agents' actions *and* constrains their discretion.[5] Giddens argues that structure is best viewed as an ongoing process rather than a thing existing "out there." He uses the term *structuration* to describe this process.

The theory of structuration provides a critical conceptual building block for my model. The idea of an enduring structure that results from our actions but also constrains our actions is central to the life cycle of commitments model. I use the term *success formula* rather than structure, however, because managers often confuse the term *structure* with a firm's organization chart.[6] Reporting relationships among business units are indeed a component of the success formula, falling within the category of relationships. Success formula is, however, a much broader notion referring to an organization's set of resources, strategic frames, recurring processes, ongoing relationships, and normative values that endure over time and place. Scholars in the fields of strategy and organizational theory have used a variety of terms to describe similar ideas, including *deep structure, institution, archetype,* and *quantum organization*, to list just a few of the more influential terms.[7] Unfortunately, none of these terms captures the exact components of the success formula. To avoid confusion, I have found it easier to use a new term: the *success formula.*

Giddens defines structure as consisting of rules and resources. These are very abstract categories, and even academics have struggled to understand what they mean in practice.[8] The success formula points to five specific components: shared strategic frames, organizational processes, resources (e.g., brand, technology, and specialized facilities), relationships, and values. These five categories emerged from an iterative process of interpreting my case study data while simultaneously reading and digesting the existing theoretical literature on commitments and inertia.[9] The resulting categories are grounded in relevant theory and powerful in explaining my case study data. The categories were also selected for their intuitive appeal to managers.

The theory of structuration clearly argues that people can shape structures. Scholars who have drawn on this theory, however, have tended to downplay people's ability to alter existing structures.[10] The life cycle of commitments model brings individuals' actions back to the foreground by emphasizing the role of managerial commitments without ignoring how commitments shape later action. The focus on managerial commitments also provides insight into how structures emerge in the first place (defining commitments), why they persist over time (reinforcing commitments), and how people can change them when necessary (transforming commitments).

FIGURE 2-1

A Company's Success Formula

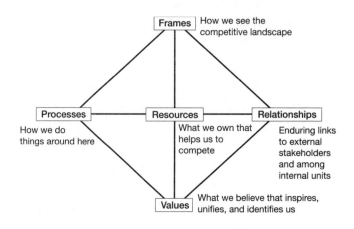

If a formula facilitates initial success, it can attract customers, employees, investors, and imitators. This positive feedback reinforces management's belief that they should fortify and extend their recipe through additional investments that reinforce the formula. With time and repetition, people stop considering alternatives to their formula; they take it for granted.[11] The individual components of the success formula grow less flexible: Strategic frames become blinders, resources harden into millstones, processes settle into routines, relationships become shackles, and values ossify into dogmas. The linkages among the components tend to tighten as well.

Once a company has stabilized its formula, it generally attracts and promotes employees who preserve stability rather than firebrands who might shake it up. A geographic concentration of firms in an industry—such as tires in Akron, cars in Detroit, publishing in New York City, or dot-coms in Silicon Valley—increases the odds that firms will concoct similar formulas that reinforce or even accelerate this entrenchment. Managers' subsequent commitments tend to reinforce their tried-and-true formulas.

An established formula serves a company well as long as the competitive, technical, and regulatory contexts remain stable.

FIGURE 2-2

The Active Inertia Trap

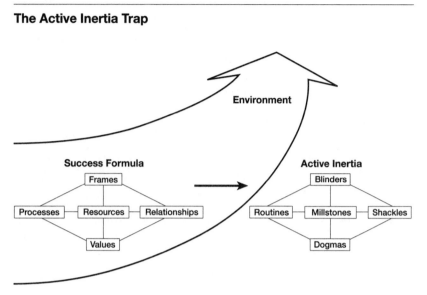

When these contexts shift, however, a gap can grow between the demands of the competitive environment and the benefits of the existing success formula. Managers see the gap, often at an early stage, and respond aggressively to close it. Their ossified formula, however, channels their efforts into well-worn ruts. The harder they work, the wider the gap becomes. The result is active inertia. Figure 2-2 depicts this cycle.

The rest of this chapter illustrates how a company's initial success formula can harden and lead to active inertia. For clarity, each of the following examples showcases the limitations of a single component—for example, strategic frames becoming blinders. But in reality, two or more components tend to hinder progress simultaneously.

Strategic Frames Become Blinders

Strategic frames, you will recall, are the mental models that shape how managers and employees interpret their competitive landscape.[12] These models answer key strategic questions, such as "What business are we in and who are our most dangerous competitors?" Frames provide focus, allowing managers to identify critical pieces of information and recognize how new data fits into a broader pattern. While frames enable managers to see, they can also blind them. By continually focusing on the same aspects of business, frames can constrict managers' vision, blinding them to novel opportunities and threats beyond their normal periphery. As their strategic frames grow more rigid, managers often force-fit surprising information into their existing mental model or ignore it altogether.

Consider the National Westminster Bank of England, the result of the 1970 merger of two long-established British banks.[13] The National Westminster network of retail banks extended throughout Great Britain; only a handful of employees were located outside the United Kingdom. Top executives of the newly formed bank committed to a clear set of strategic frames:

- Bigger is better to compete with larger rivals.
- Retail banking is stagnant and growth requires diversification.
- The United Kingdom is suffering irreversible decline and the most promising opportunities may be offshore.
- Barclay's PLC (the London-based leader) is our most important rival.

Throughout the 1970s and early 1980s, National Westminster managers boldly committed to these strategic frames: National Westminster opened branches in France, Germany, Spain, and other European countries; entered the United States with a major acquisition in 1979; and built operations in the Far East and the Union of Soviet Socialist Republics (U.S.S.R.). Back in Great Britain, management introduced new financial services, including mortgage lending and a broader range of investment banking offerings.

In 1988, National Westminster's efforts paid off as the bank surpassed rival Barclay's in assets. Outsiders lauded National Westminster managers for their bold commitments and growth. But at the same time, cracks were emerging in the bank's strategy. The deregulation of England's banking markets in the mid-1980s (known as the "Big Bang") increased competition in financial service markets. National Westminster executives responded to this regulatory change by accelerating their diversification into investment banking. But their forays were not entirely successful, and certain executives faced criminal charges in the wake of one investment banking deal gone bad. Meanwhile, competition surged in the U.S. and European markets.

In the face of heightened competition, some of National Westminster's rivals—most notably Lloyds TSB Group PLC—began cutting their losses in offshore and diversified banking to refocus on their domestic retail business. National Westminster executives, however, clung to their strategic frames—and put more chips on the table. In 1988, the company acquired the First Jersey Bank to boost its presence in the United States, but ended up losing more than $350 million on its investment. Despite conspicuous setbacks in investment banking, National Westminster continued to acquire investment banks.

The 1990s were tough for National Westminster (renamed NatWest Group in 1995). Critics blasted managers in 1995 for waiting too long to divest NatWest's U.S. operations. In 1997, Barclays reclaimed its lead in asset size and outperformed NatWest in profitability. In 2000, the Royal Bank of Scotland acquired NatWest in a hostile takeover.

When strategic frames harden into blinders, people tend to "fight the last war." Military historians have documented this tendency well. Look at the evolution of French military doctrine over the course of the last century.[14] Before World War I, the phrase *offensive à outrance*—roughly, "attack to the limit"—summarized France's military policy and framed battles as struggles of morale. Whoever displayed more *cran*, or "guts," would prevail.

But in World War I, Germany's entrenched forces easily minced waves of French troops. French military leaders learned a very costly lesson—that a guts-driven offense loses to an entrenched defense every time—and subsequently adopted a defensive doctrine, manifested in the Maginot Line, a 150-mile string of heavy fortifications built to repel future German attacks. Stuck now in this defensive frame, French military leaders ignored critics like Charles DeGaulle who argued that fixed fortifications would not defend against Germany's innovative mobile artillery. As a result, the German Blitzkrieg strategy—its offensive use of both tanks and aircraft—shredded the French defense.

Resources Harden into Millstones

Resources, you will recall, consist of both tangible assets, such as factories or equipment, and intangible assets, including brands and technology. To the extent that they are durable, specialized, and illiquid, resources lock a firm into a course of action. A company that owns valuable resources can enjoy a steady stream of profits from them, much as a landlord earns rent for the use of a building she owns.

Shifts in the competitive environment, however, can devalue established resources. Major airlines such as United, Delta, and American, for example, historically competed on the strength of their hub-and-spoke systems, in which the carriers controlled valuable real estate at hub airports and connected passengers through these centers en route to their final destination. Airline deregulation, however, opened the industry to upstart carriers who offered direct flights on heavily traveled routes. By offering low-price flights, airlines such as Southwest, JetBlue, easyJet, and Ryan Air have snatched a large share of traffic on high-volume routes and depressed prices, diminishing the value of hubs. In September 2002, the market capitalization of Southwest Airlines exceeded the combined value of the six largest competitors.[15]

When the environment shifts, a company's existing resources can contribute to active inertia. Managers hesitate to reconfigure their resources for fear of jeopardizing the associated profits. Abandoning established resources also forces managers of incumbent companies to restart from scratch, often behind start-ups with a first-mover advantage. Finally, resources often mold the company's strategic frames, processes, relationships, and values in ways that contribute to active inertia.

Consider the IBM Corporation.[16] Founded in 1911, IBM rose to industry dominance in 1964, when management introduced the 360 line of mainframe computers. The 360 line of fully compatible mainframe computers allowed customers to trade up, much like General Motors' strategy of migrating customers from Buicks to Cadillacs. Chairman Thomas Watson Jr. bet the company on the 360—investing $5 billion (the largest privately funded project to that point) and rendering the company's existing product line obsolete. The gamble paid off. By the end of the 1960s, IBM was the most profitable company in the world, with a dominant share of the U.S. market for computers.

The company invested in a set of resources that created a competitive fortress. IBM built five specialized factories to manufacture parts for the 360 line, rather than simply assembling and selling the systems as it had done in the past. IBM also spent $500 million in R&D on hardware and software for the 360. For decades, the company committed billions of dollars more in R&D and manufacturing facilities to support the 360 and its successors. These commitments reinforced IBM's strength in mainframes.

The company's huge investment in technical and manufacturing resources shaped the other elements of IBM's success formula. Prior to the 360, IBM excelled as a marketing company that solved customers' problems. After the 360, IBM's strategic frame shifted from that of a service company to a producer, as employees and managers began to see Big Blue as a maker of the "heavy iron," which contributed the lion's share of the company's profits. IBM's organizational chart also shifted and grew to reflect dense interrelationships among product components. IBM honed its sales process to sell mainframe systems to data processing managers within large enterprises. Together, these strategic frames, relationships, and processes supported the company's base of technology and production resources, further solidifying its success formula.

Big Blue minted money for decades until the law—Moore's Law—caught up with it. Gordon Moore, cofounder of Intel Corporation, predicted that microprocessor power would double every eighteen months. More powerful microprocessors made for lower-priced machines—first minicomputers and then personal computers (PCs). The proliferation of smaller products, the rise of individual consumers, and the explosion of competitors that specialized in parts like operating systems, chips, or software applications eroded IBM's hegemony in integrated systems. In this brave new world, many of IBM's customers now sought solutions to stitch all these pieces together.

Meanwhile, IBM kept focusing on big iron, but not because managers missed market changes or stood still. IBM invested heavily in PCs, launched its first product in 1981, and dominated the market within a few years. However, many IBM employees viewed PCs as "bait" to catch customers for mainframes. In the late 1980s, IBM restructured, downsized, and adopted process improvement programs. But these maneuvers were designed to use IBM's existing resources more efficiently rather than address customers' changing needs. IBM's customers grew more frustrated, and the company's performance deteriorated, culminating in cumulative losses of $16 billion between 1991 and 1993.

Processes Lapse into Routines

Processes, like frames, constitute a critical element of a company's competitive formula. Recall that processes refer to how an organization does business, both formally and informally. When a company tries something new, employees usually experiment with several ways of completing the activity. Once managers find a process that works well enough, they usually stop experimentation and commit to what worked. Deciding on a process frees people's time and energy to do other tasks and confers productivity gains as employees gain experience. Agreed-upon processes also provide the predictability required to coordinate activities within a complex organization and across the company's boundaries.

As managers standardize operating procedures, these routines resist change. Some obstacles are completely rational, such as the costs of switching procedures after installing, learning, and integrating a process into a company's operations.[17] With repetition, processes become second nature; people stop thinking of them as a means to an end, if they think of them at all, and stop considering alternatives to these comfortable, reassuring routines. When the environment shifts, managers' commitments to existing processes trigger an actively inert response.

Consider the fate of Compaq Computer Corporation in Houston, Texas.[18] In 1982, Rod Canion along with two other senior executives from Texas Instruments Inc. (TI) in Dallas sketched on a placemat a rough design for a PC with a handle like a briefcase. Frustrated by TI's approach to the PC industry, Canion and his colleagues founded Compaq and recruited several other TI managers to help them market the first portable computer. They targeted their twenty-eight-pound luggable machine at corporate "road warriors" who required a PC whenever they traveled. Compaq priced its computers at rough parity with IBM machines, but differentiated its product through higher quality. IBM sold some PCs directly to corporate customers through its own sales force. Compaq, in contrast, sold exclusively through retailers such as ComputerLand and Sears Business Center.

Compaq's high-quality clone strategy fueled explosive growth, and the company racked up revenues of $111 million in 1983, a record for first-year sales—and largely at IBM's expense. Stuck in its mainframe formula, IBM lacked capacity to fill orders for PCs. By 1986, Compaq moved beyond cloning to take the technical lead and introduced a computer running on Intel's 80386 microprocessor before IBM issued a comparable product. Compaq achieved $1 billion in revenues in record time, and achieved *Fortune* 500 status. Eight years after its founding, the company booked sales of $3.6 billion, employed more than ten thousand employees, and sold through more than three thousand resellers.

Canion and his colleagues committed to a series of processes that supported Compaq's high-quality strategy. For example, they designed the manufacturing process to ensure quality, speed products to market, and adjust the mix of goods quickly. Product cost was a distant fifth priority. Product development began with specifications that guaranteed the highest level of quality, which then drove the rest of the design. Claiming that managers aspired to be right 100 percent of the time, Canion and his colleagues also established a decision-making method throughout the company that achieved this certainty by forcing employees to attend to every detail and work the issue until all participants agreed upon the proper course of action.

Compaq's quality-at-any-price processes served the company well in the early days of the PC industry, when customers worried about the product's usability and low-cost alternatives were rare. By the early 1990s, however, hardware and software had improved considerably, and consumers began focusing on price. As the industry moved toward commoditization, new competitors entered the market. In 1991, five of the eight largest U.S. computer manufacturers followed a low-price strategy. Dell Computer advertised prices 20 percent to 40 percent lower than Compaq's for a comparable machine—a price gap approaching $2,000 for a notebook computer. Price wars depressed average industry profit margins from 8 percent of sales in 1990 to 2 percent of sales one year later, hitting Compaq's bottom line hard. In 1991, the company failed to meet analysts' earnings expectations for the first two quarters, suffered its first-ever quarterly loss in the third quarter, and announced a round of layoffs. It also announced plans to launch a single inexpensive product—*more than a year later*.

Compaq managers' commitment to customary routines channeled their response to declining profits into active inertia. Ignoring existing evidence, they gathered and analyzed more data to determine whether temporary factors such as a weak economy and a strong dollar accounted for the fall in profits. In the meantime, their well-honed new product development process cranked out highly engineered products. The manufacturing process churned out machines of the highest quality, still priced to gather dust on dealers' shelves. Faced with this ineffective response, board chairman and venture capitalist Benjamin Rosen replaced Canion with Eckhard Pfeiffer, who committed the company to serving the entire market with low-priced machines.

Note that a continual reliance on ad hoc processes can also contribute to active inertia. Just look at start-ups: Many entrepreneurs succeed early on not by instituting procedures but by continuously improvising to address volatile circumstances. As the new venture gains traction, however, the founders must instate more systematic practices to increase the internal efficiency and external reliability needed for steady growth and long-term profitability. Otherwise, these freewheelers find themselves reinventing the wheel or spinning their wheels rather than building hearty companies.

Relationships Become Shackles

In addition to frames, resources, and processes, managers commit to relationships of two kinds: *external* ones with customers, investors, governments, suppliers, and partners who provide access to critical resources that the company does not own; and *internal* reporting relationships among business units, such as those embodied in an organization chart. Managers commit to these relationships through a variety of mechanisms. They invest in technology or facilities to, for example, serve a particular customer, write long-term service or licensing contracts, form joint ventures or industry consortia, or integrate operations through acquisition, to name a few. These relationships can make or break a company—think of Microsoft and Intel, Wal-Mart and Procter & Gamble, or Firestone and Ford.

Over time, however, unchanging relationships can turn into shackles that limit an organization's flexibility and lock it into active inertia. Established relationships with customers can prevent firms from responding effectively to changes in technology, regulations, or consumer preferences.[19] Japanese beer-maker Kirin Breweries, for example, moved slowly to produce trendy new brews for younger drinkers to avoid alienating its core customers, the older generation of lager lovers.

Relationships among a company's units can also ossify.[20] For example, during the 1930s, Henri Deterding, a strong leader and Nazi sympathizer, dominated Royal Dutch/Shell and exerted his control though a highly centralized organization.[21] Shell's other executives ultimately forced him out, but the painful episode imprinted a strong distaste for centralized control. To prevent another Deterding from again amassing such power, Shell's executives established independent, highly autonomous country operations. The resulting decentralized structure enabled Shell's local operations to seize growth opportunities quickly. Over time, however, the structure hardened into a loose alliance of regional fiefdoms. When oil prices fell during the 1990s, the decentralized structure hindered Shell's top managers from consolidating operations to cut costs.

Few cases better illustrate how relationships can become shackles than the rise and fall of South Korea's Daewoo Group.[22] Kim Woo-Choong founded the Daewoo Industrial Corporation in 1967 with five employees and an initial capitalization of $10,000. But Kim had great aspirations for his enterprise—the name Daewoo means "great universe" in Korean. Thirty years later, Daewoo had fulfilled its founder's global ambitions, with consolidated revenues approaching $20 billion, approximately two hundred thousand employees worldwide, and more than four hundred and fifty overseas subsidiaries in businesses ranging from semiconductors to shipbuilding.

Daewoo grew so extraordinarily due to its close relationships with the South Korean government. Staging a military coup in 1961, General Park Chung-Hee took over the government and ruled with an iron hand until his assassination in 1979. General Park had studied under Kim's father and wanted to help his teacher's son. Under Park, the South Korean government supported Daewoo and other favored *chaebol* with subsidized financing, tariff protection, export licenses, permits for capacity expansion, and tax breaks. In exchange, the government required Daewoo and the other *chaebol*—family-controlled conglomerates—to invest in industries targeted for expansion. Daewoo dutifully obliged, expanding first in exports, then in heavy industry, shipbuilding, chemicals, automotives, semiconductors, and consumer electronics, as the government targeted each for growth. Daewoo emerged as one of South Korea's major conglomerates roughly a decade after its founding.

When General Park was assassinated in 1979, major shifts in the political and regulatory climate threatened Daewoo's position. Subsequent governments opened South Korea's product and capital markets to the outside world and dismantled much of the infrastructure that favored the *chaebol*. Chinese competitors pressured them from the low end of the market and Japanese firms from the high end.

Chairman Kim responded aggressively, expanding Daewoo assertively—some critics said recklessly—as if the government would intervene should these bets lose. Instead of loosening ties with government, Daewoo tightened them and invested heavily to build and acquire production and marketing capacity in developing countries such as China, Vietnam, India, the Sudan, and several nations in Eastern Europe. Chairman Kim forged tight bonds with local politicians to secure favorable trade and investment terms. In Uzbekistan, for example, Daewoo received a free factory site and tariff protection in exchange for a large investment in automobile production; commentators joked about renaming the country "Daewooistan."[23]

Kim borrowed as much as $47 billion to fund his investments, exceeding the foreign national debt of countries such as Poland and Malaysia. Local governments could guarantee loans but not consumer demand for Daewoo's products. By the mid-1990s, several of Daewoo's operations were running well below capacity. Rather than retrenching during South Korea's recession in 1997, Kim kept investing in expansion until the Daewoo group collapsed under its debt. The Korean government intervened—not to save Daewoo, but to dismantle it. Chairman Kim fled the country to avoid criminal prosecution.

Values Ossify into Dogmas

Entrepreneurs and managers often commit to a strong set of values for several reasons. Strong values can elicit fierce loyalty from employees, strengthen the bonds between a company and its customers, attract like-minded partners, and hold together a company's far-flung operations. Apple Computer Inc.'s global network of dedicated distributors, for example, rallied around the company's elegant systems and antiestablishment posture to create a globally recognized brand.

As companies mature, however, their values often harden into rigid rules and regulations codified in thick employee handbooks. Outdated dogmas slowly replace the once-living values until they oppress rather than inspire, and their unifying power degenerates into mindless conformity. The result, once again, is active inertia, as was the case with Laura Ashley Ltd. in Fulham, England.

Laura Ashley spent much of her childhood in rural Wales and most of her adult life recreating the charm of the English countryside.[24] Ashley founded her eponymous company in the 1950s to make and sell flowery garments of natural fibers that call to mind images of an English baroness at her country estate. Ashley adamantly denied she entered business to make money; rather, she sought to defend traditional values against free sex, hard drugs, and miniskirts.

Laura Ashley's commitment to traditional values of modesty and moderation resonated with many women in the 1970s and 1980s. The business grew from a single silk screen in Ashley's

London flat into a major retailer with an international network of five hundred shops, revenues exceeding $200 million in the mid-1980s, and a globally recognized brand. Ashley manifested her values through her maternalistic policy of providing generous pay and benefits to workers in the company's manufacturing and distribution complex located in Carno, Wales. While labor unrest crippled much of British industry during the 1970s, Laura Ashley's Welsh workers would voluntarily drive from Wales to London on their own time to deliver merchandise. Ashley also fostered close relationships with her many loyal franchisees.

When Ashley died in 1985, her husband and cofounder Bernard Ashley honored his wife's commitments. But fashion changed. As more women entered the workforce, more demanded practical, professional attire, not Laura Ashley's romantic garments. Competitors publicly dismissed the Laura Ashley style as better suited to milkmaids in the 1880s than female CEOs in the 1980s. At the same time, apparel production was changing. As trade barriers fell, fashion houses moved manufacturing offshore or outsourced it entirely to slash operating costs. Laura Ashley, in contrast, continued to pursue the outdated designs and expensive Welsh manufacturers that had served the company well in the past.

Bernard Ashley and the management team recognized their major challenges—an outside consultant had identified and reported them in the late 1980s. The board of directors, chaired by Bernard, launched a flurry of initiatives to increase sales and cut costs. The board went through six CEOs in an eight-year period, but none of them successfully refreshed the company's values to suit the modern marketplace. The company's decline continued; and, in 1999, U.S. televangelist Pat Robertson joined the board, prompting one financial journalist to wonder whether the company sought divine intervention.

This chapter introduced the concept of active inertia and explained how it arises when the elements of a company's success formula harden. Although active inertia is common, detecting it is difficult. Managers rarely notice when their success formula has so ossified that it hinders them from responding effectively to change. How, then, do you know whether management's past commitments are trapping *your* company? Chapter 3 describes some warning signals and diagnostic tests for assessing your own company's susceptibility.

THREE

Is Your Company at Risk?

A CTIVE INERTIA IS INSIDIOUS. In the euphoria of initial success, managers rarely think about their success formula, let alone consider its increasingly callused condition. When things start to go wrong, a competitive formula that worked in the past is often the last place managers look for the source of problems. Managers, moreover, lack the perspective to see their success formula clearly and impartially. They take their company's established frames, resources, processes, relationships, and values so for granted that they become blind to the need for change.

Given these difficulties, how *can* managers recognize when their organization is suffering from active inertia? One solution is to use the diagnostic tools in this chapter. The next section lists those factors that can increase managers' attachment to their success formula, thereby increasing the company's risk of slipping into active inertia. The subsequent section provides two diagnostic tests for identifying the specific frames, resources, processes, relationships, and values that might be locking the company into a rut. Last, the chapter lists some common traps that hinder organizations from adapting to changes in the environment.

These tools can supplement the company's strategic planning process, which typically addresses the obvious questions—What is happening in the environment? What are the major threats and opportunities? What should we do?—but not the most critical one: *What hinders us?*

Here, my research findings surprised me: Managers generally see major shifts coming and often even understand what they must do to prepare and to respond. The company nevertheless falters. This realization hit home for me after an offsite strategy session with a major European technology company. During our daylong session, one executive had been visibly frustrated, so I cornered him over cocktails and asked what was wrong. After the usual disclaimer—"Nothing personal, *but*"—he proceeded to explain that the session was basically wasting his time. "We have discussed all of these challenges before, and I have a set of consulting reports in my office that detail the problems and recommend a clear set of actions. We know what we should do," he continued, "so, the really interesting question is, why haven't we already done what everybody knows we should do?"

The tools described in this chapter should help managers to answer this question, ideally by incorporating these tools into a company's strategy process and using them to identify barriers to change within the organization. By stepping back to examine their company's current frames, resources, processes, relationships, and values, managers will likely cease the ineffective activity. More important, they can commit publicly to steps that will overcome whatever hinders their organization.

Risk Factors

Are the conditions inside your organization ripe for active inertia? One quick way to tell is to check the number of risk factors that apply to your situation. Each of the following factors can reinforce a manager's grip on selected frames, resources, processes, relationships, and values, thereby hampering the ability to change when the environment shifts. If your company has only one of these risk factors, then you should be fine. Two to three risk factors, and you should be nervous. Four or more, and your company is at risk for active inertia.

1. *Your company boasts superior performance.* "Pride goeth before destruction, and a haughty spirit before a fall," goes the proverb.[1] Updating this adage for modern business, we might say that excess profits goeth before the failure. Superior financial performance relative to competitors can put a company at risk for active inertia in several ways.[2] First, superior performance can lead to a sense of satisfaction with the status quo and dull managers' motivation to change. Superior performance also increases managers' confidence that they have found an effective formula for competing, that they need not search for alternatives, and that they can stick with it even when the environment shifts. Finally, high performance generates the cash flow that enables managers to continue in their current trajectory without outside financing. This internally generated cash removes one important check and balance that otherwise would prevent a manager from using a success formula beyond its sell-by date.

2. *Your CEO appears on the cover of a major business magazine.* On January 12, 1998, a beaming Eckhard Pfeiffer graced the cover of *Forbes* magazine as the CEO of Compaq, which *Forbes* editors had named Company of the Year. One year and four months later, the Compaq board of directors asked Pfeiffer to resign. The Compaq case, it turns out, was not an isolated example. Of the seven companies that *Forbes* has chosen for the honor since 1996, four have underperformed their relevant industry stock index by at least 10 percent (the other

three tracked their market benchmark), three replaced their CEO before the retirement age, and three have either been acquired by or merged with another company.[3] Table 3-1 summarizes the post-award performance of recent *Forbes* Company of the Year winners.

This "cover curse" does not indicate a lack of editorial insight at *Forbes*, a highly respected business journal founded in 1917 that now enjoys the second-highest circulation among U.S. business journals.[4] Rather, the cover curse results from a flawed assumption about the longevity of success. *Forbes* editors selected the companies based on their "staying power" and looked for companies "with clear strategies and the discipline to stick with them."[5] Their selection criteria favor managers who have committed repeatedly to their firm's clear success formula. As we have seen, this approach succeeds well in stable competitive contexts but induces active inertia in more dynamic markets. Timing also works against the company of the year. By the time a company's success formula has won critical acclaim, managers should be rethinking it, rather than gold-plating it into dogma.[6]

TABLE 3-1

Forbes Company of the Year and Subsequent Performance

Year of Award	Company	CEO Leaves Before Retirement Age	Stock Performance versus Industry Benchmark
1995	Hewlett-Packard	Yes	Underperformed
1996	Chrysler	Yes	Underperformed
1997	Compaq	Yes	Underperformed
1998	Pfizer	No	Tracked
1999	UPS	No	Tracked
2000	Charles Schwab	No	Underperformed
2001	Harley-Davidson	No	Tracked

Praise from the business press reinforces managers' attachment to the success formula in several ways. Like superior financial performance, media accolades can increase managers' self-satisfaction. Good press also bolsters their belief in the current success formula's unique efficacy and in their own personal ability to manage, and their reputation may afford them wide latitude from their board of directors.[7] Media coverage also publicly marries managers to a specific success formula and decreases their ability to switch to a new approach.

At the extreme, media attention can give rise to *hubris*. Hubris is a state of excessive self-confidence that can lead managers to disregard early warning signals of trouble or even persist in the face of changes, confident in their ability to succeed.[8] The observation that success breeds hubris, which in turn leads to failure, is far from new. Ancient authors used the phrase "drunk with hubris" to describe the state of mind that causes people to act recklessly, if not fatally. (Box 3-1, "Hubris and the Rise and Fall of Ancient Empires," summarizes some lessons from classical authors.) Of course, some prominent leaders, including Warren Buffet, Bill Gates, and Andy Grove, have received media accolades without letting it go to their heads. However, favorable press coverage—even though it attracts new investors, new customers, and new partners—remains a risk factor.

3. *Management gurus pronounce your company as outstanding.* Just as magazine editors refer to the cover curse, business academics have long observed the "guru jinx," which occurs when leading management thinkers single out a company as outstanding. When Thomas Peters and Robert Waterman published their path-breaking book, *In Search of Excellence*, in 1982, they identified a set of U.S. companies that had excelled over the preceding decade. Subsequently, several of these companies—including Digital Equipment, Kodak, Wang Laboratories, and

Hubris and the Rise and Fall of Ancient Empires

THE RISE AND FALL OF empires has intrigued historians for thousands of years. The third-century B.C.E. historian Polybius asked:

> Who is so worthless or lazy that they don't wish to know how the Romans in less than fifty-three years have succeeded in subjecting nearly the whole inhabited world to their sole government—a thing unique in history.[9]

That's what we academics call a good question. Historians observed that Rome's dramatic rise and fall had played itself out among earlier empires, including the Persian, Athenian, Spartan, and Macedonian empires.

Early attempts to explain this pattern of rise and fall resorted to a crude biological analogy.[10] All living things are born, flourish, and then die. Why should states be any different? The Greek historian Herodotus made a breakthrough, however, when he moved beyond *describing* how empires rise and fall to *analyzing* the root causes. Herodotus introduced a simple dynamic in which success breeds *hubris,* or extreme arrogance. Drunk with hubris, the successful person or state oversteps the boundaries of prudence or decency to commit an act that brings about their ultimate fall.

Hubris can cause leaders to overstep the bounds of prudence, as the story of Croesus illustrates. Croesus was the king of Sardis, which occupied land in modern-day Asia Minor. Emboldened by a string of successful campaigns against smaller states, Croesus pondered whether to wage war on the Persian Empire, which was growing stronger with every passing year. Before attacking the Persians, Croesus consulted two oracles that foretold he would destroy a mighty empire if he attacked. Overjoyed by the oracles, Croesus attacked the Persian army, but soon met with defeat. Croesus retreated back to his home base of Sardis, which ultimately fell under the siege. After leaving his vanquished city in chains, Croesus chastised the Delphic oracle for giving flawed prophecies. The oracle replied that Croesus had no right to complain. She predicted that Croesus would destroy a mighty empire if he attacked the Persians, and he did—his own. A prudent king would have made a follow-on inquiry as to which empire the oracle meant, rather than interpreting the original prophecy in the best possible light.

Hubris can also lead people to overstep the bounds of decency in dealing with others. The Greek historian Thucydides documented the Peloponnesian war, which triggered Athens' downfall as an imperial power.[11] Athens built its empire by forging alliances with weaker city-states and initially displayed tolerance toward its weaker allies. When the city of Mytilene revolted, for example, the Athenians punished only the leaders of the rebellion and left the other citizens unharmed.

As Athenian power grew, however, its leaders fell prey to hubris and made displays of power against their allies. When the island of Melos turned toward Athens' enemy Sparta, the Athenians exercised a new policy. They defined justice as "that which superiors impose and the weak accept," and argued that harsh retaliation is the only way to keep resentful allies in line.[12] Consistent with their harsh policy, the Athenians executed all the Melian men and enslaved the women and children. Rather than keeping her allies in line, Athens' growing harshness and high-handed approach turned allies toward Sparta and contributed to Athens' downfall. Industry leaders such as Microsoft and Intel might read Thucydides with interest.

How can managers avoid the hubris that often accompanies success? Here, too, ancient writers provide guidance.

1. **Recognize that success gives rise to hubris.** We all know this, but it's easy to forget at the height of success.

2. **Distrust success.** When the Roman general Scipio Africanus defeated Hannibal in the decisive battle of the Punic wars, he responded not with a great speech celebrating his victory, but with tears. Scipio would have doubtless agreed with Andy Grove's modern maxim that only the paranoid survive.

3. **Remind yourself of hubris.** A triumph was the highest honor a Roman general could receive for military conquests—no modern-day ceremony approaches it. The victorious general marched through the city of Rome behind an elaborate parade of his troops, vanquished enemies, and exotic animals brought back from conquered nations. As the general rode through the city cheered by the entire nation, however, a young boy stood behind him chanting "memento mori, memento mori"— Latin for "remember you are mortal." At the very pinnacle of a general's success and glory, the chant reminded him of his limits. Successful managers today would benefit from a similar refrain.

Kmart—suffered high-profile declines, leading *Business Week* to publish its famous "OOPS!" cover.

These gurus were not the first business academics to jinx their subjects. Nearly a century earlier, a prominent English economist, Alfred Marshall, studied the leading textile firms in Lancashire and cutlery companies in Sheffield to discover what factors contributed to their success.[13] He published his findings in an influential book, *Principles of Economics*. Over time, however, Lancashire's textile mills and Sheffield's cutlery firms suffered prolonged and painful declines.

The explanation for the guru jinx is *not* that these findings were based on sloppy research or that the companies' success was all smoke and mirrors. On the contrary, these examples represent excellent managerial writing. The authors based their findings on well-designed and executed research, and their fresh insights positively influenced academics and practicing managers. The problem with the guru jinx, like the cover curse, lies in the underlying assumption that the showcased competitive formulas will work in perpetuity. Gurus' attention also reinforces a manager's link to a competitive formula and confidence in its efficacy.

The guru jinx raises an apparent challenge for my own research. Although I am no guru, my research does single out companies as successful examples of corporate transformation. What will prevent them from suffering difficulties in the future? I fully *expect* the successful companies in my sample to encounter problems eventually. In fact, the life cycle of commitments model explains the relapse. To foreshadow an insight from chapter 8, the transforming commitments that a manager makes to break from active inertia *at one point in time* can themselves harden into a constraining new formula. Recall how IBM's commitment to the 360 locked IBM into an inexorable trajectory. According to my model, in dynamic markets *nothing is "built to last."* Rather, major shifts in the environment periodically force managers to make new commitments in order to revive their organization.

4. *You build monuments to your success.* It was said that Augustus—the first Roman emperor—inherited a city of brick and left a city of marble. During his tenure, Augustus built hundreds of bridges, aqueducts, and buildings. Many historians believe that his reign marked the pinnacle of Rome's greatness. It was—in very broad historical strokes—all downhill from there. Modern business executives rarely furnish entire cities, although executives at companies such as Firestone, Kodak, Ford Motors, Hershey

Foods, and Corning, to name a few prominent examples, certainly came close. More often, however, executives satisfy their "edifice complex" by erecting elaborate new corporate headquarters. Like Augustus' building programs, these headquarters can mark the beginning of corporate decline.

Of course, not every firm that builds a new headquarters falls victim to active inertia. Microsoft, for example, has continued to perform brilliantly after building an elaborate campus. Building a grand corporate headquarters, however, can signal that management has declared competitive victory and wishes to commemorate its triumph. Executives who memorialize their success rarely question the commitments that enabled their success in the first place.

Building an elaborate corporate headquarters can also lock a company into a community—a double-edged sword. Hershey Foods' tight links to the company town of Hershey, Pennsylvania, may have benefited the company in its early days. Community resistance, however, limited the company's ability to sell itself to a larger competitor, which might have improved Hershey's competitive position. Finally, erecting enduring buildings makes a strong symbolic statement. By literally "setting commitments in stone," building projects signal permanence and continuity that may inhibit managers' ability to rethink and reverse their former commitments. The nondescript office building in Silicon Valley can quickly adjust to new tenants, whereas the corporate monument can easily outlast the corporation, making a mausoleum of the coliseum. Instead of "building to last," maybe we should think more about "building to sublet"?

5. *You name monuments after your success.* Rather than building grand monuments themselves, executives can pay to name existing structures. Prior to 1990, only two U.S. major league sports venues were named after corpo-

rations, and two after entrepreneurs. Can you name them? (See endnotes for the answer.[14]) Since then, corporate naming of professional sports venues has increased dramatically. Like building a new headquarters, naming a football stadium or an ice hockey rink sometimes signals a susceptibility to active inertia. High-flying technology companies PSINet, CMGI, and Network Associates all purchased naming rights at the height of their success but subsequently fell on very hard times. Nor is this only a dot-com phenomenon. Compaq Center hosts the San Jose Sharks, Ericsson Stadium the Carolina Panthers, Conseco Fieldhouse the Indiana Pacers, and Enron Field the Houston Astros.

Obviously, not every company with a branded stadium or arena suffers from active inertia. Coors, Pepsi, Staples, Qualcomm, Raymond James, and Federal Express all appear to be doing fine. Nor can we blame active inertia for all the problems that a company with a branded sports venue faces. We can attribute the woes of United Airlines (Chicago Bulls), American Airlines (Miami Heat), Continental Airlines (New Jersey Nets), Air Canada (Toronto Raptors), and America West (Phoenix Coyotes) partly to the unforeseeable terrorist attacks of September 11, 2001. Naming a sports venue, however, is another red flag that sometimes signals success has gone to managers' heads.

6. *Your CEO writes a book.* CEOs don't always build monuments to their success; sometimes they write them instead. Daewoo's Kim Woo-Choong, for example, summarized his management philosophy and Daewoo's success formula in *Every Street is Paved with Gold*.[15] Kim's book sold more than one million copies in 168 days, which secured its place in Korea's *Guinness Book of Records* for the fastest book to do so. Other prominent CEO authors include John Scully, David Kearns,

and Gil Amelio. In writing a book—or an article for
that matter—an executive both articulates his success
formula explicitly and commits to it publicly. Backing
away from such an enduring public commitment
is hard.

7. *Your top executives look alike.* When radials entered
the U.S. market, the top management team at Firestone
looked "like a bunch of clones," according to an outside
executive. Recall that all had spent their entire career at
Firestone, two-thirds were Akron born and bred, and
one-third had followed their fathers' footsteps into leadership positions in the company. A homogeneous group
of top managers will likely select and promote more
managers based on their commitment to the company's
existing success formula.[16] A team of very similar managers will reinforce each other's commitments and struggle to envision alternatives.[17]

We can easily write off Firestone's gum-dipped management team as a relic of a bygone era with little rele-
vance to the current economic climate. Studying and
working with companies overcoming active inertia,
however, I have repeatedly noted the homogeneity of
top management teams. These executives share not only
demographic characteristics, such as age, gender, race,
and nationality, but also professional backgrounds. The
top management team at Compaq in 1990, for example,
consisted of several engineers who had previously
worked for Texas Instruments. In 1998, 61 percent of
Daewoo's senior managers had graduated from Seoul
National University and 30 percent had graduated from
the same high school.[18]

The quickest clone test? Just look around the room at
your next executive meeting—and board meeting, for
that matter. You can pose the series of questions in figure
3-1 to assess the number of similarities among your top
managers. No answer to any of these questions is inher-

FIGURE 3-1

Do Your Managers Look Alike?

- What percentage is male?
- How many carry passports from outside your company headquarters?
- How many attended the same university? The same high school?
- What is the average age?
- How many fall within three years of that average?
- How many rose through the ranks of the core business?
- How many worked at the same company prior to joining your firm?
- What percentage of their career have they spent with your company?
- How long have they been with your company?
- How many rose through the ranks of the domestic operations?
- How many were born and raised in the same city?
- How many speak the same language as a mother tongue?
- How many dress the same?
- How many physically look the same?

ently wrong. Rather, the frequency of identical answers puts your company at risk for active inertia. You wouldn't mistake the Compaq top management team for Daewoo's, but each team suffered because the players thought and viewed the world too much like one another.

8. *Your competitors all have the same zip code you do.* In some cases, not just one company but an entire community of firms latches onto the same success formula.[19] Some of Firestone's Akron-based competitors, for example, initially responded to radial tires just as Firestone did—by extending the existing technology and maintaining redundant manufacturing capacity. Several South Korean business groups in addition to Daewoo went bankrupt when the environment changed. In fact, history provides numerous examples of once-thriving industrial clusters that suffered when the business context shifted dramatically:

- Akron, Ohio (tires)
- Detroit, Michigan (automobiles)

- Jura, Switzerland (watches)
- Lancashire, England (cotton textiles)
- Pittsburgh, Pennsylvania (steel)
- Route 128, Massachusetts (minicomputers)
- Seoul, South Korea (conglomerates)
- Sheffield, England (steel)
- Swansea, Wales (copper smelting)

Geographic concentration can actually increase the risk of active inertia for firms within a cluster. We often think of industrial clusters as dynamic centers of innovation—for example, Hollywood's entertainment complex, New York and London's financial and publishing centers, and Silicon Valley's electronics industry (at least prior to the dot-com bust). Clusters do provide benefits.[20] They bring together talent and supporting institutions, such as specialized suppliers and investors with industry expertise. Think of Silicon Valley venture capitalists, for example, or Detroit's automobile suppliers. Geographic concentration can also promote the rapid transfer of knowledge across firm boundaries. There are no secrets in Hollywood, according to an industry adage, and there are darn few in Detroit, Wall Street, or London's financial district. The spillover of knowledge allows institutions to adopt and improve rapidly upon one another's innovations. Consequently, the firms within the cluster can produce a steady stream of innovations in products, services, and processes.

Like long-married couples, however, firms within a cluster grow to resemble one another over time. Managers in clustered firms get their information from the same sources. They read the same newspapers, closely monitor the moves of local rivals, hear the same gossip, and talk to one another to interpret what they hear. This shared information leads competition to converge on similar strategic frames and adopt comparable processes. Shared values pressure managers to conform to "how we do things around here." Convergence on similar success formulas reassures managers that they are doing business the right way. Convergence also deprives managers of a diversity of success models to apply when circumstances change.

This risk is particularly acute in secluded one-industry towns like Detroit, Akron, Jura (home to Switzerland's watch cluster), and Japan's Sakai Township (a base for the machine tool industry). Executives in an industry that dominates a locality have fewer sources of fresh ideas. One of Silicon Valley's great strengths is its diversity of industries, including semiconductors, software, nanotechnology, and biotechnology. Product-based clusters are also more susceptible to inertia than service-based ones. Manufacturing products, such as steel, tires, automobiles, and textiles, requires large capital investments in specialized production facilities and processes; modifying these resources and processes is equally costly and painful. The underlying product technology, moreover, is more susceptible to its own life cycle as innovations disrupt established products. Wall Street investment banks, in contrast, seldom lock into specialized resources.

Diagnostic Tests

If you think that active inertia is a threat, run the two quick and straightforward tests in this section to identify the specific frames, resources, processes, relationships, and values that may be jeopardizing your company. You may prefer to incorporate these diagnostics into the strategic planning process at your firm. First, however, consider the following practical tips on administering them.

The Who and How of Diagnosing Active Inertia

- *Who should conduct the analysis?* Although an individual manager can do these tests alone at her desk, a group of eight to ten managers can run them more quickly and accurately. The ideal group, in my experience, is diverse along three dimensions: (1) It consists of various levels across the organization, including top executives, seasoned middle managers, and some junior managers closest to the front lines; (2) it includes managers from both the core business in the domestic market and the peripheral businesses and global operations; (3) it mixes grizzled veterans intimately familiar with the company's history and new executives with fresh perspectives. Recent hires—preferably still in their first year—from other companies or industries can provide valuable insights and relative objectivity.

- *When should you conduct these exercises?* In my experience, managers find these diagnostic tests most enlightening when conducted outside the daily grind—an analysis of active inertia tacked on to a quarterly budget review will almost certainly fail. An offsite strategy meeting, in contrast, provides the break—physically and psychologically— from the very routines that may shackle participants. These active inertia diagnostics work particularly well at the beginning of such a meeting to kick off a broader discussion about the company's situation, obstacles to change, and alternatives for the future.

- *How should you conduct the diagnostics?* Discussions of whether a company suffers from active inertia and what the sources might be can quickly heat up. Some participants may be very vested in the success formula and may have helped to formulate it. Genuine differences of opinion will arise about whether to reinforce, modify, or scrap the current formula. An outside facilitator can help harness the emotion and strong points of view without letting them derail the discussion. The ideal facilitator will have experience leading this kind of discussion but no bias toward a specific viewpoint.

The "What Hinders You?" Test

Companies trapped by their success formula waste a lot of time, effort, and money analyzing and deliberating. They commission consulting reports, debate the conclusions and implications, and then conduct more analyses, without solving the underlying problems. The power of the "What hinders you?" exercise lies in asking a fresh question. Instead of asking "What should we do?" and then playing the same tape over and over, this exercise assumes that managers already know what to do. The discussion can then focus on what is preventing the company from doing what everyone agrees needs doing. This question, in turn, surfaces the deep sources of inertia.

The key to making this exercise succeed is to agree on what the company should do. The facilitator can do this by asking everyone to assume the board has just hired a new CEO who knows the company but is not tied to the existing success formula. Each participant—or each group, if participants work in small teams—then writes down three bullet points listing what the new CEO should definitely do. The teams should take *only five to ten minutes* to agree on the new CEO's to-do list. The compressed time prevents participants from arguing about details and forces them to focus on high-level actions. The small teams then reconvene and the entire group consolidates the proposed plans of action.

Participants might dismiss this exercise as highly artificial—no new CEO could set an action plan in such a complicated, uncertain environment so quickly. In my experience, however, the opposite more often occurs. To their surprise, participants quickly reach a rough agreement on a few key actions that the new CEO should take.

At this point, the group can discuss why the company has not taken these actions already, going through each agreed-upon action one by one and exploring the obstacles to executing them. The categories of strategic blinders, millstones, routines, shackles, and dogmas can help organize participants' responses. To prevent the discussion from drifting into broad generalities, the facilitator should focus participants on the specific obstacles to the concrete actions that the new CEO should take. I often pose the question, "If the new CEO tried this, then what would happen?"

The "Vito Corleone" Test

This diagnostic exercise borrows its name from a scene near the end of the first *Godfather* film. In this scene, the dying Vito Corleone (Marlon Brando) sits in the garden with his son Michael (Al Pacino) and advises him how the Corleone dynasty could fall after his death. Vito predicts that the rival Mafia families will attempt to assassinate Michael. He warns his son that the rival families will lure him into a trap by sending someone that Michael trusts to escort him to a meeting with the other dons. The critical insight from this scene? Danger lies not in an unexpected ambush by an unknown perpetrator but in a betrayal by a trusted party.

A company's cherished success formula can also lead managers into great danger. This exercise is intended, like Vito Corleone's advice to his son, to identify the known and trusted as sources of danger. The group can begin by systematically discussing the firm's critical success factors to date, in terms of strategic frames, resources, processes, relationships, and values. Figure 3-2 provides detailed questions to guide this discussion.

After identifying the critical frames, resources, and other commitments that constitute your company's success formula, the group then looks at how these might contribute to active inertia going forward. For a realistic appraisal, go through the items on the list one by one. Assume that each item on the list will definitely constitute a source of active inertia. The group can discuss how the scenario might play out. Of course, the individual frames, resources, processes, relationships, or values that the group identifies may never cause problems in the future. Managers should

FIGURE 3-2

Questions to Identify Your Company's Historical Sources of Success

Strategic Frames

Which of your assumptions have been critical to your success?

- Who are your most important competitors?
- What competitors can you afford to ignore?
- What is your strategy?
- Which are your critical customers?
- Which markets are key?
- What industry are you in?
- How do you get to market?
- Which customers can you safely ignore?

Resources

What does your company own that creates value?

- What does your brand mean to customers?
- Which elements of your technology are critical to your success?
- What facilities enable you to succeed?

Processes

Which of your organizational processes—both formal and informal—have been most critical to past success?

- New product development
- Hiring
- Decision processes
- Manufacturing
- Customer service
- Capital budgeting
- Executive promotion
- Service delivery
- Logistics (supply chain management)

Relationships

Which of your external and internal relationships account for previous success?

- Distributors
- Providers of capital
- Government agencies
- Providers of complementary goods or services
- Local communities
- Outsourced activities
- Suppliers
- Employees
- Collaborators
- Alliance partners
- Standards boards

Values

Which shared values have unified and inspired your company in the past?

- What does your company stand for?
- What company is totally *unlike* yours?
- What is your company against?
- Which values make you so different?

exercise this diagnostic tool to understand how the specific elements of their success *might* impede adaptation.

Common Traps

While conducting the diagnostic tests, managers should stay alert to common traps that emerge across different industries, geographies, and historical eras. The seemingly positive statements in the following sections are examples of these potential pitfalls.

Strategic Frames Become Blinders

- *We are a growth company.* Managers often extrapolate past trends to forecast future growth. Changes in the competitive context can render these forecasts irrelevant, but managers are often slow to see the discontinuity. Firestone's managers knew radials lasted twice as long as the existing tires, but still forecast growth. High-tech leaders such as Cisco and Siebel may have fallen into the same trap when demand for information technology slowed.

- *We know our competitors cold.* A clear focus on a single competitor can limit managers' peripheral vision. Compaq's focus on IBM kept managers from recognizing quickly enough the threat posed by low-cost clone makers such as Dell. National Westminster's executives' focus on Barclays reinforced the bank's ill-fated strategy of global diversification. When everyone in the company agrees on the same competitor, it may be time to get nervous.

- *We are number one.* A single-minded focus on market share can trap a company in active inertia. The Swedish manufacturer SKF, for example, led the global ball-bearing industry in market share through much of the twentieth century. When Japanese competitors threatened SKF's dominance, management responded with aggressive capital spending and marketing to win share. Managers' strict focus on market share obscured their attention to profits and led them to take on marginal business. A fundamental rethinking of the strategy to pursue profitable segments might have proved a better option.

Resources Harden into Millstones

- *Our brand means the product.* For many consumers, Xerox means photocopying, Kleenex equals tissue, Hoover means vacuum, and Lego stands for plastic blocks. An airtight link between a company's brand and its product provides a powerful marketing edge over rival offerings. When the market shifts, however, the brand name can hinder managers from repositioning the brand or extending it beyond the core product.

- *We have it all.* Over time, companies often weave a dense web of specialized operations to support their core business. Recall how Firestone integrated backward to produce rubber and tire components and forward into retail stores. Shifting the core business would require untangling this dense web of specialized assets.

- *Our technology is a fortress.* At its peak, Xerox protected its core photocopier technology with more than five hundred patents. Sitting behind such a strong technical garrison, Xerox managers initially dismissed the simpler copiers offered by Canon and Ricoh.

Processes Lapse into Routines

- *We have a "bible" for critical processes.* Managers sometimes codify the steps in a critical process in a manual. Codification allows managers to capture what they learn from experience, apply it efficiently, and communicate it throughout the organization. This manual can become the "bible" for a critical process. Banc One and Cisco Systems, for example, codified their successful acquisition programs. A bible, however, is hard to change. The codified process can take on a life of its own, and employees can continue to follow it even after the environment has shifted.

- *We hire and promote people like us.* Firms suffering from active inertia often have a team of homogeneous executives at the helm. Many of Compaq's top executives came from Texas Instruments, and Firestone managers were "gum-dipped." This uniformity was no coincidence. These executives were the products of management selection and promotion processes that produced a standard product. Elimination of variance to the six-sigma level is desirable in manufacturing. In management promotion, however, it deprives a company of the diversity of views necessary to respond effectively to change.

- *We make our decisions by consensus.* Consensus decision making works extremely well when a few people have the luxury of time to get to the "right" decision. The bad news is that the right decision too late is often the wrong decision, and consensus decision processes can proceed at a glacial pace. A common active inertia story unfolds when a company that made decisions by consensus in the past—such as Compaq—enters a fast-moving market or watches its traditional market grow more turbulent. Managers respond to accelerated pace and increased uncertainty with the same consensus process that served them so well in the past. Unfortunately, it produces decisions that are too late or too timid or both.

Relationships Become Shackles

- *We know our place in the value chain.* Managers in many successful companies can pinpoint their company's position in the industry's value chain. Compaq, for example, owed much of its success to strong ties to resellers who aggressively promoted the company's PCs. When the competitive environment changes, however, profits may shift to different points along the value chain or new competitors may configure themselves in different ways. Dell surged ahead of Compaq (as well as Hewlett-Packard and IBM) in the PC market by selling direct to consumers. When booming Internet sales later reinforced the advantages of Dell's direct sales model, Compaq struggled to copy Dell's model, fearing a backlash from its established distributors.

- *We do the important tasks in-house.* A related trap occurs when a company has a strong bias for doing everything in-house. Laura Ashley managers, for example, insisted on manufacturing all products in Wales long after competitors had moved production offshore. Even when managers recognize the benefit of focusing on a core set of activities, they still encounter difficulties in disentangling themselves from operations traditionally done in-house.

Values Ossify into Dogmas

- *We are a family, not a company.* Companies often espouse a set of shared values to forge a community that makes the corporation more than a mere legal entity. When these unifying values harden into family values, however, they may limit managers' ability to make tough decisions that would harm the interests of "family members." Firestone executives delayed closing unnecessary factories at least in part to protect the interests of employees and host communities. Laura Ashley managers maintained expensive production facilities in Wales out of loyalty to the employees "in the family." Of course, managers should not ignore loyalty or corporate responsibility, but recognize the risks associated with "family values" in a corporate setting.

- *We have a campus, not a headquarters.* To attract talented employees in a tight job market, companies such as Apple and Trilogy Software enticed candidates with promises of a campus rather than a stuffy headquarters. A campus implies academic values, including informality and the independence to pursue one's own interests. These values can harden into a sense of entitlement that every employee should be free to pursue any project of interest. Complete independence hinders managers from redeploying employees to new projects that may cut costs and boost profits but lack sex appeal.

- *Our competitors are our enemies.* Red-blooded managers harbor a healthy competitive streak. When rivalry hardens into hatred and competitors become enemies, however, companies can be lured into active inertia. Managers at Apple Computer, for example, viewed IBM as the evil empire that stood for everything that Apple employees hated—conformity, bureaucracy, and dull gray boxes. Recall Apple's Orwellian ad during the 1984 Olympics. Even Apple's motto "think different" contradicted IBM's slogan "think." Apple's anti-IBM ethic may have slowed employees' ability to recognize the threat posed by Microsoft.

This chapter has provided a set of warning signals, diagnostic tests, and common symptoms of active inertia. What do you do if the tests come back positive and you believe your company is suffering from active inertia? The good news is that this malady is not always fatal. It can be overcome through transforming commitments. The bad news is that these commitments are not appropriate in every circumstance. The next chapter discusses transforming commitments and when they are right for a company.

FOUR

The Power of Transforming Commitments

ACTIVE INERTIA CREEPS UP like a receding hairline. But unlike hair loss, managers often fail to notice just how "actively inert" their company is. Difficult as it is, diagnosing active inertia is far easier than changing an established success formula. An organization's historical commitments to strategic frames, resources, processes, relationships, and values—individually congeal with time. Tight interdependency among these elements reinforces the solidity of the formula as a whole. Success reassures managers that they have found the single best way to compete. Over time, the company—and probably its competitors—takes the formula for granted. A cadre of like-minded managers reinforces it and deprives executives of potentially valuable alternatives. Monuments like buildings and books publicly link successful managers to their proven formula. Given all the forces hardening a company's success formula, how can managers ever change their own?

The answer is through transforming commitments, the third stage in the life cycle of commitments model. We have already seen an example of transforming commitments in action: Goodyear altered its formula to compete when the environment shifted. This chapter first helps managers to decide whether their organization needs transforming commitments and then walks them through the three steps of transforming the company's formula.

What Are Transforming Commitments?

Transforming commitments are actions that remake an organization's success formula by increasing the cost (or eliminating the possibility) of persisting in the status quo. Managers, as we have seen, instinctively respond to changes in their environment by working harder. But the company's history, as embodied in its success formula, channels their actions down well-worn routes. To surmount active inertia, managers must explicitly commit to transforming their organization's success formula.

Consider Asahi Breweries, created in 1949 when the Japanese government split Dai Nippon Breweries in half to promote competition.[1] Asahi became one of Japan's "big four" brewers thereafter, along with Suntory, Sapporo, and market leader Kirin. Each of the four industry leaders offered its flagship lager to a set of loyal core customers, mostly Japanese "salary men." These drinkers had grown accustomed to the lager rationed to Japanese troops during the Second World War. By the 1980s, however, a new generation of beer drinkers had come of age. Market research revealed their preference for a sharper-tasting beer than traditional lager. Fearing a backlash from their core customers, the big four brewers delayed offering new products. Asahi's response to changing consumer tastes was a classic case of active inertia. Managers made incremental changes to product packaging (e.g., introducing a "mini-barrel"), redoubled their established sales and marketing efforts, and tried to cut corners by using cheaper ingredients.

In 1986, Hirotaro Higuchi—a banker at Asahi's lead bank, Sumitomo—joined the company as president. Higuchi understood Asahi's competitive position and realized that the company could never succeed by cutting costs while selling its traditional lager to an aging segment. Instead, Higuchi broke ranks with Asahi's competitors and committed to providing a new beer for the younger generation. Higuchi launched Asahi Dry, a sharp break from the company's established lager line. Higuchi invested heavily in the new product launch and pulled the old beer from the shelves. Younger drinkers loved Asahi Dry instantly. Between 1986 and 1990, before he knew whether dry beer was an enduring category or a passing fad, Higuchi upped the company's capacity fourfold. This investment—which exceeded the book value of the company's assets at the time—was a bold bet on a risky new direction.

Many managers might have hedged their bets by rolling out dry beer gradually or leaving the existing beer on the shelves. Higuchi knew, however, that only bold actions would provide sufficient counterweight to the gravitational pull of Asahi's existing success formula. Higuchi's subsequent commitments prevented Asahi from continuing on its trajectory. If dry beer failed, then the company could fail. This bet forced the organization to modify its new product development and brewing processes as well as its relationships with distributors. Higuchi's big bet paid off. Young drinkers stuck with Asahi Dry, and the brewer caught up with and ultimately overtook market leader Kirin, while its stock subsequently outperformed the Japanese brewing index. Figure 4-1 depicts Asahi's rise.[2]

Higuchi's bet on dry beer illustrates a critical aspect of transforming commitments—they are bold. Timid managers do not pull an established product off the shelf and quadruple capacity in advance of demand. Higuchi's actions positioned Asahi well relative to competitors. Dry beer also provided a neon-bright alternative to the company's established success formula of selling lager to aging drinkers and cutting costs to boost margins. Like the proverbial general who burned his bridges behind him, Higuchi

FIGURE 4-1

Kirin and Asahi Share of Japanese Beer Market: 1971–2001

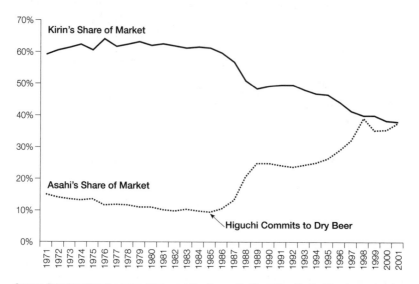

Source: Data from Timothy James, "Resource Development in Firms: New Product Development and Organizational Change in the Japanese Brewing Industry," (Ph.D. diss., University of Washington, 1992), table 5.8.

blocked Asahi employees from retreating to their comfort zone. So bold commitments can both position a firm for a prosperous future and transform its previously winning formula.

But bold commitments also entail risk. Had dry beer proved a fad, Higuchi's bet would have failed. Recall New Coke. The risk of transforming commitments stems from two sources: First, the new formula might not work out as planned. Second, the transformation might destabilize the core business and jeopardize a predictable profit stream.[3] Transforming commitments leave a company particularly vulnerable because they simultaneously set out on a new direction while destabilizing the core of the business. Transforming commitments present a dilemma. They must be sufficiently bold to break with the gravitational pull of the established success formula, but bold commitments do entail risk. How can managers decide whether the potential reward of a transforming commitment is worth the gamble?

Transforming commitments are a sort of Rorschach test that reveals much about a manager's attitude toward risk. Some managers see only the downside and choose to *avoid* the risk inherent in transforming commitments. They bury their heads in the sand and perpetuate stale actions. Other managers, in contrast, see only the upside of bold bets and often *ignore* the associated downside risks. Blinded by optimism, they rush into the fray. Prudent managers, however, have a third option. They can actively *manage* the downside risks while realizing the benefits of transforming commitments. The first step is deciding whether your company needs a transforming commitment.

Are Transforming Commitments Right for You?

Transforming commitments are not a panacea. They are the business equivalent of strong medicine. They can work wonders but also have serious side effects. Prudent managers should not enter such a treatment lightly. Many factors, including the company's financial cushion, competitors' likely response, and management's ability to lead such a transformation, influence whether transforming commitments make sense in a specific situation. I have found two factors, however, that are particularly important in deciding whether a transforming commitment or an alternative treatment is more appropriate. First, does the change in the environment threaten your company's core business? Second, does your company have a good alternative to the status quo? The interactions of threat and alternatives and the recommended actions are depicted in figure 4-2.

When does a shift in the environment threaten a company's core business? Radial tires dominated the traditional technology on every dimension that mattered to consumers, and incumbent tire firms that failed to switch faced ultimate extinction. As aging lager customers were replaced by a new generation of drinkers, Asahi faced competitive irrelevance. Not every change in technology,

FIGURE 4-2

Are Transforming Commitments Right for Your Company?

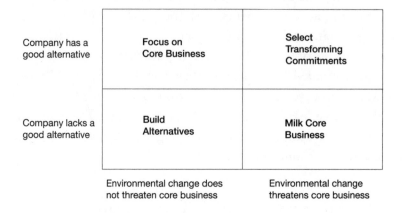

	Environmental change does not threaten core business	Environmental change threatens core business
Company has a good alternative	Focus on Core Business	Select Transforming Commitments
Company lacks a good alternative	Build Alternatives	Milk Core Business

consumer preferences, or regulation, however, threatens a company's core. At the height of the dot-com bubble, it was predicted that industry after industry would crumble in the face of online upstarts.[4] A few industries have, indeed, been clobbered by online competitors—think travel agents, music, and brokerages. Traditional competitors in many segments, however—including business-to-business exchange, grocery shopping, retail banking, insurance, and targeted retailing—are still standing while their challengers have come and gone.

You can ask a few simple questions to assess whether a change in regulation, technology, competitive dynamics, or consumer tastes would threaten your core business.

- Are your current customers demanding change?

- Have your most finicky customers already migrated to new rivals or incumbents who altered their success formula?

- Can you spin a scenario in which the change bankrupts your company?

- Can you picture an alternative scenario in which the change proves irrelevant?

- Of the two scenarios, which disturbs managers more?
- What do your investors or creditors think?
- Has market value shifted toward entrants with a different model?
- Are investors comparing your company unfavorably to such entrants or to traditional adversaries who have already transformed their success formula?

If most of your answers unnerve or dishearten you, then the change likely threatens your core business. None of these questions is a perfect indicator of a company's vulnerability. Recall the astronomic valuations assigned to companies like Chemdex and Webvan during the dot-com bubble. When considered together, these questions can prompt managers to view their environment more realistically.

The second dimension to consider is whether a company has a good alternative to its success formula. Good alternatives take two forms. Companies with multiple divisions may have a promising business unit outside the core.[5] Managers can transform the company by shifting its center of gravity from the historic core to a promising peripheral one. Intel, for example, could exit its memory business because it had identified microprocessors as a lucrative alternative. In these situations, transformation consists of making a formerly peripheral business the new core of the company. Managers can change *what* the company does. Managers can also transform *how* the company competes within its established core business. Here, a good alternative means a manager can retain some elements of the success formula, rather than blowing it up and starting from scratch. Asahi committed to younger drinkers, a big bet to be sure, but continued as a beer company, used the same distributors, and retained close ties with Sumitomo Bank. A bad alternative, in contrast, would have required Asahi to fundamentally change everything all at once.

Now let us turn to the matrix in figure 4-2. If your company has good alternatives and faces no immediate threat, then put yourself in the upper left-hand quadrant and focus on your core business while preserving your strategic options against future shifts in the environment. Procter & Gamble, for example, is focusing on its core lines while maintaining new product R&D.

The lower left-hand quadrant depicts a situation in which your company does not face an immediate threat to its core business but also lacks good alternatives. This generally occurs in the case of focused businesses that compete in a single market. Equity analysts refer to such companies as "pure plays" and generally praise them for sticking to their knitting. Focus has benefits, of course, but it also leaves companies vulnerable to shifts in their environment.[6] Managers who find themselves in this situation may choose to nurture and protect some new initiatives outside the core as call options against unforeseen changes in the competitive context that might arise in the future.

The most difficult situation occurs when a company faces a threat to its core business but has no good alternative (the lower right-hand quadrant in figure 4-2). Consider the case of Smith-Corona.[7] Smith-Corona was formed in 1926 through a merger of two established players and succeeded for decades thereafter as a focused player in the typewriter industry. The rise of personal computers, however, posed a clear and present danger to Smith-Corona's core. The company lacked a portfolio of other businesses that might have provided the platform for future growth. Entering the PC business, moreover, would have required Smith-Corona to start virtually from scratch in developing new processes, reframing its core business, exploring alternative distributor relationships, and repositioning the brand, which most consumers equated exclusively with typewriters.

Managers who encounter a threat to the core without good alternatives often attempt to build a new business from scratch. Smith-Corona did, for example, make an ill-fated foray into personal computers. Such crash-course efforts are likely to fail for three reasons. First, incumbent managers are generally too late to the party. An established company's strategic frames often prevent managers from seeing the new opportunity early on. Entrepreneurs unencumbered by these blinders are quicker to see and seize the opportunities. Apple Computer was nearly a decade old, for example, by the time Smith-Corona entered the PC market. Second, the new businesses must battle for scarce resources with established and profitable businesses—battles they often lose.[8] Third, the bold commitments required to transform the existing success formula are often *too* bold for a start-up. Entrepreneurs generally stage their commitments to keep options open in the face of uncertainty. Any commitments that are large and fast enough to pull a company out of active inertia are likely to be too big and too premature for a start-up.

Managers facing an immediate threat to the core with no good alternatives should avoid risky crash-course efforts to change everything all at once. Instead, managers in these buggy-whip situations should consider milking their core business and paying the proceeds to investors through dividends or stock repurchases. Managers in this quadrant might, for example, take the company private through a leveraged buyout. The resulting leverage would focus managers on extracting cash from the core business and help them avoid the temptation to reinvest in projects unlikely to earn an acceptable return. Some people view LBOs as a fad whose time has come and gone. For companies in this quadrant, however, they may be just what the doctor ordered.

Some companies *do* have good alternatives as they face a threat to their core business—they have a promising peripheral business or can respond without changing every element of their success formula all at once. This situation is represented by the upper right-hand quadrant of the matrix. Companies in this quadrant are the best candidates for transforming commitments. But where should managers begin? Transforming an organization's success formula is a complicated and messy process, particularly if the organization is large, geographically dispersed, or complex. At its essence, however, the process can be visualized as consisting of three steps, which are described in the next section.

The Three Steps to Making Effective Transforming Commitments

The process of *belaying* in ice climbing can help us visualize how transforming commitments work.[9] Picture a group of mountaineers huddled on a ledge of a steep wall of ice and striving to reach the snow-capped peak above. To scale the wall, one mountaineer climbs up and secures an anchor into the ice face. Once the anchor is fixed in place, the leader loops a rope around it and drops the rope to the climbers below. One by one, they pull themselves up to the new height, with the belay anchor and the sturdy line catching them when they slip.

We can divide the belaying process into three steps. First, the lead climber must *select* an appropriate anchor. Choosing the anchor that suits the specific situation is tricky work because it depends on the condition of the ice, the weight of the climbers, and the leader's experience with the various sizes and shapes of anchors in his rucksack. Second, the climber must *secure* the anchor in the ice so that the attached rope can support the rest of the climbers. Third, the first climber must *guide* those below, stabilizing the line to break their fall. Like making transforming commitments, belaying (and ice climbing in general) requires a combination of discipline, boldness, and self-awareness. Timid climbers would never leave their base camp, and disorderly climbers would not survive many climbs.

By analogy, you can visualize the process of selecting and securing transforming commitments as a three-step process. In the first step, a leader selects an anchor. The anchor is *what* the manager commits to. Managers can commit to a new strategic frame, process improvement, renewing the company's resource base, stretching relationships with external parties, or novel values. Different anchors have advantages and limitations as levers to pull an organization from active inertia (we will discuss their relative merits in the next chapter). Anchors provide an overarching objective to prioritize actions that keep managers from trying to change everything all at once.

In the second step, a manager secures the anchor with transforming commitments. Like defining and reinforcing commitments, transforming commitments are *actions* such as capital spending, public promises, or personnel decisions, but they differ in their relationship to the success formula: Defining commitments shape the success formula, reinforcing commitments renew it, whereas transforming commitments change it. (While transforming commitments in the narrowest sense apply only to these securing actions, I sometimes use the term broadly to describe all three steps of the process.)

In the final step, the manager realigns the organization's remaining frames, resources, processes, relationships, and values. The leader's transforming commitments create tension with elements of the existing success formula. Employees easily slip into established blinders, millstones, routines, shackles, and dogmas. In this third step, the leader must struggle against backsliding as he brings the success formula into a new alignment.

Obviously, belaying differs substantially from climbing out of active inertia. Ice climbers are there by choice. If a climb looks treacherous, then they can generally return to camp. Managers who face a threat to their core business are like climbers perched on a melting ledge of ice. They climb for their organization's life. And they need all the help that they can get.

Transforming Commitments in Action

Let's illustrate the three-step process of transforming commitments with one of the most successful transformation stories in recent business history—Louis Gerstner's tenure at IBM.[10] Gerstner was selected after several high-profile executives pulled their names from the list of potential CEOs. Gerstner joined the company in 1993, when IBM reported losses of $8 billion in a single year. During Gerstner's nine years as CEO, IBM's net income grew to nearly $8 billion in his final year as CEO. By the end of Gerstner's tenure, competitors such as Hewlett-Packard were once again struggling to look more like IBM. Gerstner's actions are a textbook example of selecting an anchor, securing it, and realigning the rest of the organization.

Step 1: Select an Anchor

An anchor refers to an overarching objective that guides subsequent actions. Gerstner's anchor was a new strategic frame—providing integrated solutions to IBM's customers rather than simply selling them mainframes. Hardly revolutionary stuff, but Gerstner's move from selling products to solving problems highlights a critical point about anchors. They need not be inspirational, novel, or audacious. Most anchors are, in fact, pretty mundane—technical leadership in the core business, serving a new generation of customers. Effective anchors must only present a clear alternative to the established success formula and fit the situation, not win any awards for creativity.

Selecting an anchor provides powerful benefits in wrenching an organization out of active inertia. An anchor provides focus and allows employees and managers to prioritize their actions. Some managers, however, fail to select a single anchor because they try to change everything all at once. The results can be unpleasant. Consider the case of Michael Spindler, who became Apple Computer's CEO the same year Gerstner joined IBM.[11] Through his early tenure at Apple, Spindler never settled on a single anchor. In his statements to the business press, shareholders, and industry participants, Spindler listed no fewer than a dozen objectives, but it was unclear how these goals were prioritized; in some cases, they appeared to be at odds with one another; moreover, they shifted over time. Of the twelve stated in major forums during his first year in office, only one—"increase market share"—appeared consistently. By the end of his first year, he had become "the fire hose" to some employees because "he moved so quickly and in so many directions spouting ideas and putting out fires."[12] This flurry of objectives disoriented employees, managers, partners, customers, and investors alike. No one seemed to know where Apple was headed.

Michael Spindler was a good manager in a difficult situation. Could anyone have reversed Apple's fortunes, given the booming Wintel standard and the company's dysfunctional culture? Not with a long list of themes. Executives and employees can pick and pursue whichever appeals to them most, dissipating their energy in different directions rather than focusing it for a real transformation. Other times confusion or cynicism sets in, and employees simply do what they have always done, until the CEO changes his mind again or gets sacked. When it comes to anchors, more is definitely not better. Business is, of course, complex and managers often have multiple objectives. A fixed anchor, however, provides both clarity and a means of prioritizing actions.

Step 2: Secure the Anchor

Selecting an anchor is a necessary first step, but only the first step. To provide the leverage necessary to pull employees out of active inertia, the anchor must be secured firmly. Otherwise, the gravitational pull of the existing success formula will drag the company back into the status quo. Managers can give their anchor traction with new commitments.

You could imagine that Gerstner's theme of providing integrated customer solutions might be generic enough to attract the ridicule of Dilbert. Putting the customer first was certainly no novel idea. Gerstner gave his anchor traction, however, through a series of concrete actions. He continuously hammered away at the same message in public forums within and outside IBM. Gerstner reversed plans to break IBM into separate businesses, dubbed "Baby Blues," because an integrated IBM would allow the company to provide customers with better solutions to complex problems. Gerstner's decision to keep IBM intact surprised many people. Many people assumed that he had been hired expressly to execute the plan to dismantle IBM, which had been set in motion by his predecessor. Gerstner also invested to support IBM's mainframe business, which many observers had written off as a goner. Again, Gerstner's rationale was clear—customers wanted the mainframe, so they would get it at a lower price and with improved technology, to boot. Gerstner's surprising actions sent a clear message that he was serious about providing integrated solutions to customers' problems rather than simply selling hardware.

Gerstner also put his time where his mouth was. By his own estimate, he spent approximately 40 percent of his time visiting customers. This stood in stark contrast to his predecessors in the top slot, who devoted much of their travel schedules to visiting IBM's own sites around the world. A few weeks after joining the company, Gerstner cleared his calendar to spend two full days at a customer conference. Based on their experience with previous IBM CEOs, employees thought they would be lucky to get one hour of the CEO's time for such a function.

Step 3: Realign the Rest of the Organization

Committing to an anchor exposes obstacles to achieving the new objective. Gerstner's commitment to provide integrated solutions surfaced a host of challenges to making good on that promise. The sales force was organized by geography, for example, and many sales executives lacked the industry expertise to solve customers' problems. Despite its breadth, IBM's product and software portfolio still had gaps that prevented the company from providing integrated solutions. A clear anchor can help managers prioritize their actions. They focus first on the most pressing obstacles to honoring their new commitments. Other issues can wait on the back burner. At IBM, executives reorganized the sales force around industry groups to better solve customer problems. IBM also invested in mainframes, acquired new software, and beefed up its internal services business to better provide integrated solutions.

One way to visualize the prioritizing function of an anchor is to picture a mobile like the ones that hang over a baby's crib.

Lying on the ground, a mobile is a tangle of string and plastic—much like the challenges facing a company mired in active inertia. If you pick the mobile up in the right spot, however, the pieces sort themselves and fall into their proper place.

Gerstner succeeded in large part because he focused ruthlessly on the details. Some executives excel at the big picture of selecting an anchor and making big bets. They are less adept, however, at managing the details required to deliver the goods. Gerstner, however, excelled at the nuts-and-bolts actions—including process improvements and cost cutting—required to make good on his pledge to solve customers' problems. Not all of these actions were easy. Cutting costs required IBM to reverse the long-cherished policy of no involuntary layoffs. A hard-nosed focus on execution, however, is every bit as necessary as the choice of anchor and willingness to strengthen it with bold actions.

The Good News and Bad News About Transforming Commitments

As with most things in life, there is both good news and bad news about transforming commitments. Let's start with the good news. Transforming commitments are a concrete tool managers can readily use. If an outside force threatens your core business but you have a good alternative, then managerial commitments can help you respond effectively. The three-step process of selecting an anchor, securing it, and realigning the organization provides a framework for answering some of the most daunting change-management questions: What should you change first? How can you make the changes hold and prevent relapses? How should you prioritize your actions? The approach here stands firmly on my analysis of companies that did successfully break out of active inertia and adapt to changes in their environment. The basic insights from these cases have been sharpened by theory and refined in the classroom. Most important, managers struggling to transform their own organizations have road-tested these tools in the real world.

Now the bad news. Transforming commitments do not work in every situation—for example, if a company faces a threat to its core and lacks decent alternatives. Moreover, they are hard work: Selecting the most appropriate anchor requires an in-depth understanding of your company's situation and the pros and cons of alternative anchors; securing the anchor demands risky commitments; realigning the organization requires constant diligence. Managers, moreover, must make difficult personal choices along the way.

While transforming commitments do not hold out the false promise of a quick and easy fix, they can succeed when properly executed. The remainder of this book provides guidance on selecting the optimal anchor for your company, securing it firmly, and realigning the rest of the organization. It is a guide for managers who have committed to the ascent.

———————

To recap this chapter's argument, transforming commitments are actions that managers take to transform their company's existing success formula. The process of making effective transforming commitments consists of three steps: select an anchor to guide the commitments, take concrete actions to secure the anchor, then realign the rest of the organization. To understand how transforming commitments differ, let's compare them with some established ways of thinking about strategy and change.

FIVE

Choosing the Right Anchor

AN ANCHOR PROVIDES the overarching theme that prioritizes a manager's transforming commitments. An anchor, secured by forceful actions, enables a manager to hoist a company from its active inertia. However, most practitioners think only about *strategy* when they first hear about anchors and, in doing so, eliminate many of their best options. As my research revealed, a new strategy or strategic frame is only one of many possible anchors, and not necessarily the best. (The transformation of Pepsi-Cola described in box 5-1 shows how a new strategy can emerge several years into a transformation effort).

In addition to strategic frames, then, what anchors can managers choose? Potentially, any of the other areas of commitment— new resources, processes, relationships, and values. Each can serve as an effective anchor, as this chapter will illustrate. For managers, then, the first question is not, "What should our new strategy be?" but "Where should I start?" recognizing that the right answer might be resources, processes, relationships, or values instead of a new strategy.

BOX 5-1

Pepsi's Challenge

FROM ITS FOUNDING in the late 1800s, Pepsi-Cola spent much of its history fighting to win market share from industry leader Coca-Cola.[1] By 1985, Pepsi-Cola had narrowed the gap with its larger rival (accounting for approximately 29 percent of U.S. soft drink volume to Coke's 37 percent) and had consistently achieved earnings growth of 15 percent per year. Pepsi faced several challenges to sustaining its increases in revenues and profitability. Growth in overall demand for cola was slowing as alternative beverages, such as bottled water and fruit drinks, gained share at the expense of cola. Private-label colas continued to dent the leaders' positions. Coke's strong distribution presence in restaurants such as McDonald's helped it win share.

In 1986, Pepsi's top management committed to transforming the company through a new relationship with its bottlers. Traditionally, Pepsi had franchised its bottlers, granting them exclusive rights to distribute the product in a specified geographic region. In the late 1980s, however, Pepsi embarked on an aggressive campaign to acquire bottlers. All told, the company invested approximately $4 billion to integrate its bottlers and increased its percentage of owned bottling capacity from 18 percent in 1983 to over 50 percent by 1990.

The commitment to a much closer relationship with its bottlers raised a host of new challenges for Craig Weatherup, Pepsi-Cola's president and CEO. Prior to the acquisition, Pepsi had served hundreds of customers—their franchised bottlers—but now found themselves serving hundreds of thousands of customers that the bottlers delivered to every day. Traditionally, Pepsi had succeeded through high-profile marketing campaigns such as celebrity endorsements by Michael Jackson, Shaquille O'Neal, and Ray Charles. Success in the bottling operations, however, required operational excellence in determining customers' needs, making the product, delivering the product, and servicing the customers.

Weatherup and his team responded to this new set of challenges first by articulating a set of values, including customer orientation, results orientation, clear expectations, and teamwork, that would be necessary to drive improvement in the bottling organization. Pepsi managers referred to this set of guiding principles as the "Right Side Up" values. To track progress toward the new goals, Weatherup commissioned surveys in which employees were asked to rate their manager's conformance to the "Right Side Up" values.

Shortly after developing the new set of values, Pepsi's top management embarked on an initiative to improve operating processes. One Pepsi top executive recalled that employees initially "rejected process thinking like an organ transplant. People said, 'We hate it, it's garbage, we're action based and it will slow us down.'"[2] Pepsi managers developed a method for mapping and improving processes, however, that mapped critical processes and initiated a best-practices program to codify and disseminate the most effective procedures throughout the organization.

It was only after they had restructured the relationship with bottlers, attempted to change values, and improved operating processes that Pepsi's executives turned their attention to strategy—nearly six years after they had first decided to acquire bottlers. In the summer of 1992, Weatherup unveiled the "Total Beverage" strategy, in which Pepsi planned to offer a preferred beverage throughout the day. The Total Beverage strategy required Pepsi to expand aggressively beyond cola and broaden its product offerings to include alternative beverages such as bottled water, ready-to-drink tea, sports drinks, and even milk- and coffee-based beverages. Pepsi managers hoped to derive one-half of planned revenue growth from alternative beverages.

The Pepsi-Cola case illustrates that managers need not begin their transformation with a new strategy—Pepsi-Cola began by committing to a new relationship with its bottlers. Rather, a new strategy may emerge as a later step in aligning an organization around a new set of resources, relationships, processes, or values.

The managers in my study eventually chose their anchor after wrestling with their companies' challenges and approaching their problems from different angles. No universally applicable, step-by-step method emerged for selecting the strongest anchor— the choice depends on too many organizational idiosyncrasies. So, rather than providing a one-size-fits-all methodology, this chapter reminds managers of their choices. It also illustrates the respective pros and cons of these various anchors and the optimal conditions for each type's success. By showing each anchor in action, this chapter should help you select the best tool for your company's situation. Box 5-2 describes how *not* to select an anchor.

BOX 5-2

How Not to Choose an Anchor

To CHOOSE AN ANCHOR, a manager must deeply understand the company's history, competitive context, and alternatives. There is no easy method for choosing the ideal anchor for your organization. There are, however, some clumsy ways of choosing an anchor that fail pretty regularly. Be wary of the following rationales.

It Worked Last Time

A hallmark of active inertia is responding to new challenges with tried-and-true actions. Recall Chairman Kim at Daewoo. Managers sometimes think three times is a charm. Three strikes and you're out is probably a better rule.

It Worked in My Last Job

Outsiders hired to transform a company often use the anchor that worked in their last job. Indeed, they're often hired to do just that. If the circumstances at the new company differ substantially, however, the anchor will probably not hold.

It Works in Theory

Outsiders often fall into another trap. They work with consultants to develop an elegant plan. They then dismiss criticism from incumbent managers as resistance to change. Recall that Jeff Skilling developed Enron's "gas bank" strategy while a consultant. The plan sounded great in theory. Outsiders need to vet their selected anchor with veterans within the company.

It Worked for Our Competition

Managers often seize the anchor used by a successful competitor. Hewlett-Packard, for example, is following IBM with its bid to provide solutions rather than boxes. But one-size anchors may not lift every company in an industry, and even the right anchor too late may prove ineffective. If your entire community of competitors is trapped in active inertia, then following someone else's lead will only spin your wheels.

It Worked at GE

The most common anchor I've seen is a new strategic frame to be number 1 or number 2 in a market. This anchor worked for Jack Welch in the 1980s. Effective anchors are not generic, but reflect a company's history and context—think dry beer. Managers can't avoid the hard work of selecting an anchor by copying Jack's paper.

Reframe Strategy

Commitments to a new strategic frame can force a sharp break with a company's historical direction. The case of Nokia's dramatic transformation from a struggling Finnish firm to a world leader in telecommunications illustrates the advantages, risks, and ideal circumstances for electing strategic frames as an anchor.[5-3]

Imagine you are a contestant on *Jeopardy*, and you select the category "famous Finnish companies" for $50. The answer (not surprisingly) is "Nokia." You respond: "Which company is the leading producer of mobile phones in the world?" You are correct. Had you been playing *Jeopardy* in the late 1980s, then you could have answered: "Which company brought electricity to 350 Egyptian villages, makes the most toilet paper in Ireland, and provides all the studded winter bicycle tires in the world?"[4]

Founded in 1865, by the late 1980s Nokia had grown into a widely diversified conglomerate producing rubber, chemicals, paper products, industrial machinery, cable, and a grab bag of electronics products. Mobile phones and telecommunications equipment accounted for less than 10 percent of total revenues, and in 1987, the mobile phone business was losing money.

Nokia suffered a series of corporate body blows during the late 1980s and early 1990s. The unraveling of the Soviet Union deprived Nokia of one of its largest customers. In the early 1990s, the Finnish government began opening the country's formerly protected market. Then came Finland's most severe recession since the depression of the 1930s. The company hit bottom in 1991, when its largest shareholders attempted to sell their stake to Swedish telecommunications rival Ericsson, which declined the offer.

In 1990, Nokia's CFO, Jorma Ollila, was assigned to the company's mobile phone division and given six months to develop a proposal on whether Nokia should sell it. After a few months on the job, Ollila concluded that mobile phones represented Nokia's future. The impending adoption of a European-wide digital cellular standard named GSM would open up a huge new market for mobile phones, and Nokia could leverage the early lead it had established in the Nordic market, which then led the rest of the world in mobile phone adoption.

When the board tapped him to run the company in 1992, Ollila developed a new strategy to transform Nokia from a Finnish conglomerate to a global telecommunications firm. To give this new strategy teeth, Ollila eliminated other options. Over the next few years, Nokia divested all its businesses unrelated to telecommunications, including legacy businesses like paper and its high-profile consumer electronics division, to fund Nokia's expansion.

Ollila and his management team realigned the mobile phone business to pursue this new strategy. They consolidated Nokia's phones under a single brand and invested heavily to build the brand globally. They revised the new product development process to design a line of phones with a common look and feel but different technical guts. They tapped a global network of suppliers and designers. Nokia also forged strong relationships with upstart telecommunications providers such as Orange in Great Britain and worked with customers in Japan and the United States to learn what consumers outside Europe valued.

The rest, as they say, is history. Nokia launched its 2100 series of phones in 1993 and projected to sell 400,000. It ultimately sold more than 20 million and emerged as a global leader in the telecommunications market. The primary advantage of committing to a new strategic frame is clarity. This clarity allows managers to communicate the new strategy throughout the organization. Nokia employees might have agreed or disagreed with the bet on global telecommunications, but they certainly understood it.

Clarity also allows managers to draw a line between what the company did in the past and what it will do in the future, which helps employees break out of historical patterns of thought and provides laser-like focus on the same future direction. The clarity of a new strategic frame also guides resource-allocation decisions. Nokia invested heavily in brand building for mobile phones while exiting unrelated businesses. Given these benefits, managers often select strategic frames as an anchor.

Bold commitments to a new strategic direction also entail important risks. If the chosen course of action fails to pan out, then a company can find itself with few options and limited resources. The Nokia story might have turned out very differently had consumer adoption of mobile telephones occurred later or more slowly. The single-minded focus on the new frame can lull managers into strategic tunnel vision in which they miss early signals that the approach isn't working. Strong commitment to a clear course of action can also lead managers to escalate their commitment in the face of negative news.

A new strategic direction works best when the company already has the foundation for the new direction in its portfolio. Nokia was already in telecommunications, Asahi's engineers had already developed dry beer. Starting from scratch, as you will recall from chapter 4, forces managers to embark on a crash course in the new business. Big bets on a new strategic direction also work best when the potential payoff is high enough to offset the inherent risk. Nokia's gamble offered the company an opportunity to establish itself as an early leader in one of the fastest-growing industries in the world. Daewoo's bet on automobile production, in contrast, offered the prospect of a small share in a cyclical industry plagued by global overcapacity, limited exit, and low margins. Finally, a manager should commit to a risky new strategy only when the alternatives are grim. With its back against the wall, Nokia had little to lose by boldly shifting its strategy.

Renew Resources

Managers can also commit to renewing their resource base to pull their organization out of active inertia. Consider the case of South Korea's Samsung Group.[5] Entering the 1990s, Samsung closely resembled the Daewoo Group we saw in chapter 2. Both counted among Korea's four largest groups, were widely diversified, and were controlled by the founding family. Samsung and Daewoo, moreover, had succeeded using nearly identical success formulas. Both groups relied on close ties to the government and both competed by achieving scale economies through quantity rather than winning through high quality. Both groups faced the challenges of diminished government support and heightened global competition.

But here the similarities end. Samsung's founder died in 1987, and his third-born son, Lee Kun-Hee, succeeded him. Skeptics doubted whether much would change. Lee Kun-Hee, after all, was his father's son and had worked in his shadow for nearly a decade before becoming chair. Lee believed, however, that Samsung required a complete overhaul to thrive in the changed environment. At the fiftieth anniversary of Samsung's founding in 1988, Lee declared a "Second Foundation." Lee argued that Samsung must wean itself off government support and compete on product quality versus quantity production. Samsung could only achieve this transformation, Lee argued, by investing heavily in resources—specifically, the group's technology and brand name. The contrast with Daewoo's response could not have been clearer. Samsung would cut government ties and build the resources required to compete on quality. Daewoo, in contrast, would expand in developing countries where the group could forge close ties with local regimes and compete with lower-quality products.

Lee was dissatisfied with the slow pace of change and in the early 1990s took several bold actions to improve Samsung's resource base. He initiated a series of meetings around the globe for Samsung's 1,800 top executives. In these sessions, managers visited electronics retail stores and saw how products made by brand leaders such as Sony received the best placement in the stores, while Samsung's products were often piled in a corner, sometimes gathering dust. To build its brand, Samsung nearly doubled advertising as a percentage of sales between 1993 and 1994 and held it at the higher level thereafter.[6]

To deliver on the brand's promise of high quality, Samsung managers invested heavily in technology. In 1999, for example, Samsung Electronics was granted more than 1,500 patents, which placed the company among the top five patent recipients in the United States that year.[7] A decade earlier, Samsung had received only twenty-six patents. Lee also committed to aligning the organization around the new resources. Samsung exited several businesses deemed incapable of ever competing on brand and technology, including commodity textiles, paper, and sugar—all-important drivers of the group's historical success. Group companies instituted a series of process improvement initiatives, including six-sigma and a line-stop program to reduce defects. In 1994, Lee publicly criticized Korean politicians for being fourth-rate in a speech widely interpreted as Samsung's declaration of independence from the Korean regime.

The results of Lee's transformation of Samsung were dramatic. Samsung emerged even stronger from the 1997 recession in South Korea that precipitated Daewoo's fall. In 2000, Samsung emerged as the largest *chaebol* in South Korea, and foreign investors favored the companies under the Samsung Group umbrella.

The Samsung case illustrates both the pros and the cons of selecting resources as an anchor. On the positive side, building a brand or developing technology confers an enduring competitive advantage that competitors cannot replicate quickly. The flip side of enduring resources is their downside: Developing new technology or renewing a brand requires sustained effort over time. Recall how Lee began his initiative in 1987, had to jump-start it in the early 1990s, and realized success only in the late 1990s. Building the resource base can cost a lot. Recall not only Samsung's investment in R&D and advertising, but also IBM's bet-the-company investment in the 360 mainframe back in 1964.

Resources work best as anchors when managers believe that they must change *how* they compete rather than *where* they compete. Samsung remained in many of the same businesses (with the exception of a few divestments of legacy businesses). Resources are also more likely to succeed when managers enjoy the luxury of time. By laying the groundwork for the transformation in the late 1980s and picking up the pace a few years later, Lee avoided the costs and risks of a crash program. Of course, not every manager has time on his side. If you do not, then you should not choose resources as the anchor for your organization.

Reengineer Processes

Managers frequently select processes as the anchor to lead a transformation of their company's existing success formula. Well-known examples include Larry Bossidy's transformation at AlliedSignal using six-sigma and Bob Galvin's renewal of Motorola by competing for the Malcolm Baldrige Award. Processes offer several advantages as an anchor. The process improvement toolbox includes several well-defined and documented techniques for improving a firm's processes, including total quality management (TQM), statistical process control (SPC), process reengineering, and six-sigma. A recent search of Amazon.com yielded 321 books on process reengineering, 132 books on total quality management, and 45 on six-sigma.[8] Prominent institutions, including the International Standards Organization (ISO) and National Institute of Standards and Technology, provide support to companies attempting to transform their company's processes. Although managers generally select operating processes as the handle to transform their success formula, they can also choose from alternative processes, including new product development, decision making, and resource allocation.[9] Since organizational processes lie largely within the boundaries of the firm, managers exercise considerable control over them.

To illustrate process as an anchor, let's turn to another Korean company, this one a small, focused supplier to the automotive industry by the name of Duck-Yang Industries.[10] Duck-Yang manufactures pads that house instruments in a car's dashboard, absorb vibration, and protect passengers in accidents. In 1994, Duck-Yang was small (670 employees), provincial, and comfortable. The company had enjoyed a cozy relationship with Hyundai Motor Corporation—its largest customer—for nearly twenty years. In the mid-1990s, Hyundai began pressuring its suppliers to improve their quality and placed Duck-Yang's crash pads on its list of the ten most defective products.

Duck-Yang managers concluded that they needed to fundamentally transform their business and chose manufacturing process as their anchor. To give their commitment teeth, they publicly pledged to achieve 100 parts per million (ppm) defect levels by the end of the following year. Employees were incredulous. Hitting the target would require a hundredfold reduction in defects. It would also place Duck-Yang ahead of even the most sophisticated Japanese parts suppliers in terms of quality.

Top management created a cross-functional team that collected data on quality defects, identified the root causes, and implemented a series of countermeasures to eliminate defects. Duck-Yang managers also guided the company's frames, relationships, resources, and values into a new alignment. By setting such demanding targets, Duck-Yang's top executives stopped comparing themselves to the best competitors in South Korea and set their sights on the best rivals in the world. Duck-Yang managers restructured relationships with key stakeholders: The company invited process improvement experts from Hyundai to coach the team and took a series of actions to improve relations with the labor union, including building dormitories for workers, air conditioning the factory, and installing a karaoke system in the employee lounge. Duck-Yang worked with its suppliers to help them improve the quality of subcomponents supplied to Duck-Yang. Executives also used process improvement as an opportunity to shift the company's values toward respect for data. The disciplined approaches for collecting, analyzing, and acting on quality data reinforced a respect for fact-based problem solving rather than the finger pointing—based on assertion and opinion—that had plagued the company in the past.

Duck-Yang's transformation was a rousing success. In 1996, Duck-Yang's defect rate for finished products dropped to 3 ppm, which Hyundai believed was the highest quality in the world. Labor productivity increased 20 percent, and in 1996, Duck-Yang's achievements were recognized when the company received the prestigious Presidential Award for Excellence from the South Korean president.

Committing to transforming processes doesn't always have such a happy ending, however. A major initiative to change processes can focus managers and employees too internally and distract them from large changes in the environment. Recall the case of Xerox.[11] When Canon and Ricoh challenged Xerox's near-monopoly in the copier market in the 1970s, Xerox managers responded by trying to beat the Japanese at their own game. Xerox managers launched a series of quality programs to improve internal processes. They adopted and adapted many total quality management tools common among leading Japanese manufacturers. Xerox did not go so far as to institute company songs, although that may be explained by the difficulty of finding lyrics to rhyme with Xerox. These process improvement programs succeeded in halting Xerox's decline in its core copier market, and articles and books with titles like *Prophets in the Dark: How Xerox Reinvented Itself and Beat Back the Japanese* and *Xerox American Samurai: The Behind-the-Scenes Story of How a Corporate Giant Beat the Japanese at Their Own Game* heralded the company's victory.[12]

But another book came out that told a very different story: *Fumbling the Future: How Xerox Invented, Then Ignored the First Personal Computer.*[13] Because of their narrow internal focus throughout the 1980s, Xerox managers failed to recognize that researchers in the Palo Alto Research Center (PARC) had opened up whole new opportunities for massive value creation. A series of other companies—including Apple, Microsoft, and 3Com—captured much of the value from PARC's innovations.[14]

Process improvement, more so than any other anchor, can also assume a life of its own. In process improvement programs, managers and employees can quickly lose themselves among the details of each step. A manager at a specialty chemical company, for example, committed to transforming his division by implementing continuous improvement in new product development and production processes. He rewarded employees for the number of suggestions they made. The manager eventually abandoned his initiative, however, when he realized that employees focused primarily on generating specific suggestions, rather than changing the culture and beating competitors.

Processes generally work best as an anchor when a manager truly believes that the company's strategy is sound but the execution plan is not. Duck-Yang managers, for example, knew what to do, but not how best to do it. Process-led transformations also work well when an outside manager wants to buy time fixing obviously broken processes while figuring out whether he needs an alternative anchor in the long term. Fixing a broken process is rarely a bad move (unless the company no longer needs it), as long as managers recognize that it alone may not suffice.

Stretch Relationships

Most managers are familiar with strategy, resources, and processes as possible anchors to transform their organization. Few, however, recognize the power of *stretch relationships*. Managers use stretch relationships by committing to leading-edge customers, demanding investors, or accomplished partners. Most managers avoid such stretch relationships because they disrupt the status quo by placing "unreasonable" demands on the organization. They fail to understand that *these very demands pull the company up from its active inertia.* By seeking out and locking their organizations into these relationships, managers can wrench their companies out of established blinders, millstones, routines, and dogmas and prevent them from lapsing into bad habits.

Managers can enter into stretch relationships with leading-edge customers. Recall, for example, how Gerstner recommitted IBM to providing solutions to Big Blue's core customers. For another example, consider Infosys, India's leading software company, which enjoyed a seventeenfold growth in revenues from 1994 to 1999.[15] The inertia of established business practices in India has historically frustrated aspiring entrepreneurs, many of whom have emigrated to pursue opportunities elsewhere. CEO Narayana N. Murthy succeeded partly by committing to relationships with leading-edge customers. Murthy's company could have made a comfortable living serving local firms. Instead, Infosys managers carefully "recruited" their customers based upon their sophistication, prestige, and potential for a long-term relationship. Infosys's client list reads like a "Who's Who" of admired companies, including General Electric and Nordstrom. Nearly all of its clients are headquartered outside of India. By committing to ongoing relationships with sophisticated global clients—rather than serving less demanding local customers—Infosys learned global best practices. Along the way, Infosys pioneered a model that other Indian companies, such as Wipro and the Tata Group, have subsequently emulated and helped establish software as one of India's few globally competitive industries.

Managers can also commit to stretch relationships with demanding investors. Consider the impressive transformation of Lloyds TSB under Sir Brian Pitman.[16] In the early-1980s, Lloyds TSB (not to be confused with Lloyds of London) closely resembled its rival National Westminster, the bank we discussed in chapter 2. Like National Westminster, Lloyds TSB had focused on getting big, going global, and diversifying outside its core business of retail banking in Great Britain. By 1983, Lloyds TSB, like its rival National Westminster, had achieved these goals.

When Brian Pitman became CEO of Lloyds TSB in 1983, his bank faced the same challenges as National Westminster. The bank's international loan portfolio was suffering from defaults in South America. Closer to home, the British government had announced their plan for "Big Bang" deregulation, which would open the banking industry to new competition.

National Westminster managers, you will recall, responded to these changes by accelerating their attempt to get big and diversify. Pitman, in contrast, broke ranks with his rival. Pitman committed to a stretch relationship with the bank's investors. Putting shareholders first may sound old-hat today, but among English bankers (and, indeed, corporate Europe as a whole in the 1980s), the notion was heresy. British bankers traditionally prided themselves on a balanced approach to serving the interests of their multiple stakeholders—including regulators, their gentlemanly competition, employees, customers, and investors (in roughly that order). Pitman believed that serving multiple masters created conflicting objectives that prevented excellence. To bring order to this confusion of constituents and objectives, Pitman committed clearly to making investors the first priority.

Pitman's commitment to a stretch relationship led him and his management team to change the bank's strategic frames. Historically, the British banks equated success with size. Pitman, however, redefined success in terms of serving shareholders. He initially set return on equity targets to measure success. A few years after becoming CEO, however, he publicly committed to a more aggressive goal and pledged to double Lloyds' market capitalization every three years. Value-based metrics were incorporated into the company's investment process and led Lloyds to make a series of surprising decisions. While National Westminster rushed to expand globally and diversify into investment banking, Lloyds closed its investment banking business and retreated from global markets. While National Westminster was deemphasizing its retail banking operations to expand abroad, Pitman was making acquisitions to grow Lloyds TSB's English customer base. For example, Lloyds broadened its consumer product line to include insurance and mortgages. In all cases, the creation of shareholder value drove Lloyds TSB's contrarian decisions; investors liked them, but employees, host communities, competitors, and the British establishment did not.

Pitman delivered. Lloyds Bank did, indeed, double its market capitalization every three years for the seventeen years that Pitman served as either CEO or chairman of the board. The company enjoyed the highest market capitalization of any of the Big Four banks. Rivals like National Westminster belatedly emulated many of Lloyds TSB's moves, exiting from volatile investment banking operations and unprofitable international ventures. Their delay cost them dearly, however.

Managers can also commit to stretch relationships with joint-venture partners. Consider the case of Japan's Nikko Securities.[17] Like Lloyds, Nikko Securities was a member of a cozy oligopoly of four financial service firms. For seventy years, Nikko—along with Nomura, Daiwa, and Yamaichi Securities—had been one of Japan's four largest brokers. Like Lloyds, Nikko faced increased competition in the 1990s resulting from Japan's own "Big Bang." The Japanese brokers also faced the country's largest post-war recession and a scandal in which industry executives were convicted of contacts with gangsters.

Unlike Lloyds, Nikko managers did not select shareholders for their stretch relationship. Instead, they entered into a partnership with another bank to drive change. In 1997, Masashi Kaneko was appointed Nikko's president in the midst of the racketeering scandal. Kaneko—a Columbia University M.B.A. who had spent much of his career in Nikko's international operations—recognized that Nikko Securities would need to fundamentally transform its established organization to compete in the new competitive environment ushered in by Japan's Big Bang. Kaneko decided that a partnership with another bank would not only shore up Nikko's balance sheet, but also provide pressure to change the brokerage. The obvious choice for a partner bank would have been the Bank of Tokyo. Nikko Securities was a member of the Mitsubishi network, and the Bank of Tokyo was the lead banker. Kaneko surprised everyone, however, by bypassing the Bank of Tokyo to enter into a joint venture with Salomon Smith Barney's Japanese operations. The new joint venture—with the unwieldy name of Nikko Salomon Smith Barney (NSSB)—would provide investment banking, sales and trading, and research services to corporate and institutional clients. Kaneko sealed the deal by selling a 20 percent stake in Nikko to the Travelers Group, which owned Salomon Smith Barney.

The joint venture exposed Nikko's insular employees to international best practices. The stretch relationship also provided pressure that allowed Kaneko to push through other changes over widespread resistance. Kaneko abolished Nikko's traditional seniority system, for example, to reward performance. He also changed brokers' established quotas to reduce churn in clients' portfolios. In contrast to the Lloyds TSB example, Nikko's transformation is still under way and worth watching to see whether Kaneko and his team will successfully harness the changes in Nikko's wholesale business to transform the retail brokerage. Regardless, Nikko's situation shows that alternatives exist when selecting a stretch relationship.

Stretch relationships offer several advantages as anchors. First, they provide an external focus. Infosys's global customers and Nikko's partnership with Salomon Smith Barney both forced employees to look outside the organization for direction on how to change. In some cases, these external partners, investors, or customers can also provide specific tools and advice to achieve needed changes. Infosys employees, for example, learned global best practices from the sophisticated IT departments within their customers' organizations. Stretch relationships also provide external pressure for change that managers can harness. Lloyds TSB's Pitman argues that the greatest advantage of committing to shareholders lies in their unrelenting demand for improvement, which keeps constant pressure on the organization. Finally, stretch relationships can provide managers flexibility in how they keep the customers (or investors or partners) satisfied. Thus, Pitman's commitment to shareholders or Murthy's commitment to meeting the needs of companies like Nordstrom or General Electric did not lock them into a specific course of action.

Stretch relationships have their drawbacks, of course. Managers can choose the wrong partner. Even if a manager chooses an appropriate stretch relationship, the new customer or group of investors can assume too much control. CEOs such as Jean-Marie Messier at Vivendi, for example, have made big commitments to shareholders and subsequently found themselves out of a job when they failed to deliver the goods. A company's most valuable customers can hijack its resource allocation process and prevent it from seizing new opportunities. Finally, negotiating during a crisis generally favors the healthier company over the besieged one;

beleaguered managers start from a position of weakness and should beware of partners who might exploit them.

Stretch relationships work well as a handle for transformation when the manager needs some external pressure that she can harness for tough calls. Shareholder value helped Pitman justify controversial disinvestment decisions, for example. Stretch relationships also work well when the manager has some means of credibly binding her organization to the partner. Managers can commit credibly to customers and investors by putting their organization in a position where it depends on these stakeholders for necessary resources. Nikko's joint venture with Travelers worked well partly because the companies bound their fortunes with equity exchanges. Many alliance partnerships, in contrast, provide little leverage for transformation because both partners can walk away at will. They amount to little more than a press release and a puff of smoke. Committing to leading customers works particularly well when the customers reciprocate to help the company develop.

Recoin Values

Values exert a powerful allure as an anchor. This choice, in my opinion, is generally a mistake. The benefits of changing values are, of course, compelling. A new set of values can energize the troops. If employees exemplify a company's core values, then executives can trust them to act accordingly without elaborate control systems. Values, like resources, also constitute an enduring source of transformation.[18]

Despite the benefits of changing an organization's values, however, my research suggests that they are the most difficult anchor. Direct attempts to change values often degenerate into generic statements of "core values" that any company in the world could adopt and that most employees will ignore anyway. Managers must change a company's values to effect an enduring shift in its success formula, but these changes are generally best achieved as a byproduct of changing the more tangible elements of strategic frames, resources, processes, or relationships. Recall how Duck-Yang's top management, for example, built a respect for data-based analysis as a part of aligning the organization around the new operating process. When managers attempt to grab values directly, they often end up with a handful of air.

Notwithstanding these difficulties, managers can select values as an anchor under certain conditions. Consider the case of McKinsey.[19] Today, the firm numbers among the world's most admired business organizations and consistently ranks among the most desired employers by M.B.A.s. In the 1930s, however, its predecessor firm—McKinsey, Wellington, & Partners—was one of dozens of fledgling accounting and engineering firms offering advice to managers. Marvin Bower, a partner in the New York office, grew convinced that an organization rooted in the firm's accounting heritage was ill suited to the demands of the new management consulting sector.

Instead, Bower drew on his own legal training to articulate a set of values based on the "professional" norms that dominated the more established fields of law and medicine. As McKinsey grew, Bower constantly reaffirmed McKinsey's commitment to the "professional approach" and guided dialogues among his partners about what professionalism meant in practice. In attracting and retaining the best staff, for example, McKinsey explicitly adopted the process of hiring and promoting freshly minted graduates through a strict up-or-out policy, pioneered originally by the law firm of Cravath, Swaine, and Moore. Bower also shifted the firm's frames and insisted on adopting the terminology common among more established professions. McKinsey had (and has) "clients" rather than "customers"; "professionals," not "employees"; and is "a firm" ("The Firm," actually) rather than "a company."

Bower's choice of values as his handle to transform McKinsey's existing success formula succeeded because a clear alternative value set, along with the associated processes, relationships, and frames, already existed in the established professions of med-

TABLE 5-1

Summary of Possible Anchors

	Pros	Cons	Works Best When
Strategic Frames	Clarity of focus Easy to communicate	High cost if big bet fails Risk of tunnel vision	An alternative is in place Payoff of bet is high Alternatives are grim
Resources	Enduring competitive advantage Difficult to imitate	Time-consuming Expensive	Strategy is sound, but execution is weak Luxury of time exists
Processes	Well-defined tools exist External institutions support Manager controls processes	May focus the organization too internally May focus too much on details of process	Strategy is sound, but execution is weak Buy time while selecting another anchor
Relationships	Provide external focus Flexibility in how to change	Could choose wrong partner Lose control Weak bargaining position	Need external pressure to change Can credibly bind the relationship Partners are committed to help
Values	Energize the troops Influence without control Enduring source of change	Can be too generic Tough to change directly Time-consuming	Clear alternative value set exists New values have broad legitimacy Luxury of time exists

icine and law. While leaders of consulting firms consistently refused to take the steps—such as professional certification—to become an "official" profession, they could draw on the underlying values of professionalism that enjoyed legitimacy among clients and employees. Bower also had the luxury of time to start with values and bring the other elements along. Bower assumed leadership of McKinsey in 1938, but it was not until the 1950s that he was able to persuade his partners to adopt the up-or-out promotion process common at law firms.

This chapter reminds managers that they have a choice when selecting an anchor. Each of these anchors has advantages, risks, and circumstances under which they work best. Table 5-1 summarizes these. Chapter 6 provides guidance on helping managers execute transforming commitments successfully.

Picking the Right Person for the Job

MANY TRANSFORMATION EFFORTS fail. Managers can, however, increase their chances of success by selecting the best anchor, as we saw in chapter 5. They can also ensure the right person is in charge. My research revealed that the person who commits to transforming an organization's formula matters nearly as much as the anchor selected and the actions taken. The best candidates share a few characteristics:

- They are familiar with the company's business without being trapped in the existing success formula.

- Their personal values and professional backgrounds are consistent with the anchor chosen and the commitments made.

- They don't try to do it all themselves, but rather surround themselves with a strong and diverse team.

- They have the necessary support, tenure, and incentives to succeed in this leadership role.

If these criteria don't fit, then it's dangerous to undertake the transformation. This chapter explores each of these considerations so that (1) managers can determine whether they themselves are cut out for the daunting task of transforming the corporation, (2) company directors, trustees, executive search committees, or senior managers can more prudently identify, screen, and select promising candidates to lead a do-or-die transformation, and (3) the manager and the compensation committee can structure the right deal.

The Power of Inside-Outsiders

When a company is locked in active inertia, the board often hires outside managers to break from the past. Recall that, after decades of success, Firestone's gum-dipped managers responded to radial technology by doing more of the same. When performance deteriorated to an alarmingly low level, the board brought in an outsider with turn-around experience to bring a fresh perspective to Firestone's success formula.[1]

The outsider wasted no time. Within his first three months, he closed five of Firestone's fourteen domestic tire factories, severed ties with established customers and distributors, and reversed long-standing commitments to the Akron community, all irrevocable actions that broke sharply with Firestone's past. He also imposed a top-down strategy and investment process and staffed key posts with outsiders. His dramatic actions saved Firestone from bankruptcy.

Problems emerged, however, when he attempted to shift from his cut-and-restructure mode into a growth mode. Despite objections from seasoned managers, the "outsider" divested Firestone's most promising peripheral businesses—thereby irreversibly depriving Firestone of its platforms for profitable long-term growth. Worse, the new CEO bet big on retail stores, despite glaring evidence that company-owned stores had not earned acceptable returns in decades.

After an initial burst of high performance, Firestone lagged the tire industry in stock performance and attracted two hostile takeover bids. The Japanese tire maker Bridgestone eventually acquired Firestone, which continued to limp along under this new ownership.

The failure of Firestone's outside CEO to transform the business after the turnaround illustrates some of the limitations of outsiders. They lack familiarity with a company's operations and industry that could improve their decisions about what to change and what to leave alone. "You've got to know when to hold 'em," to quote the song made famous by Kenny Rogers, and "know when to fold 'em, know when to walk away, know when to run."[2] Outsiders often lack this insight and can make poor—and often irreversible—decisions as a result. Absent a deep understanding of their new context, outsiders often do what worked for them in their last job, heedless of the new situation's demands. Firestone's outside CEO, for example, invested in retail stores based on his consumer electronics experience, where controlling the distribution channel yielded attractive returns.

Outsiders may also lack—or fail to establish—credibility with the old guard, who may subvert the new manager's agenda. While this problem did not afflict Firestone, it certainly affected Apple, where engineers and middle managers undercut every outsider's efforts to revamp the corporate culture. Finally, outsiders may not yet have developed trusted inside advisors who can help to overcome the old guard's resistance and avoid poor decision making.

Thus, selecting the best person to transform a company's existing success formula poses a dilemma.[3] Outsiders bring fresh perspective and freedom from historical commitments, allowing them to act quickly and decisively. Insiders, in contrast, possess the deep knowledge for choosing wisely and the credibility to get things done. Which one should we pick? Here's one possible solution: Find "inside-outsiders," my expression for managers within

the company but outside its traditional core business. Contrast
Firestone's outsider with Goodyear's Chuck Pilliod, an Akron
native who had spent his entire career with Goodyear. He worked
twenty-nine of his first thirty-one years in the company's international division, where he witnessed the rapid adoption of radial
technology in Europe. When he became president, Pilliod already
understood Goodyear's situation, respected the company's heritage, had proven himself an adept leader, and was acknowledged
as "one of us." His years outside Akron provided the distance and
perspective of an outsider.

Inside-outsiders led several of the most successful transformations in my study, such as the turnarounds at Compaq, Nokia,
Lloyds TSB, and Asahi Breweries. Jack Welch, the best-known
transformational leader in recent business history, certainly quali-
fies as an inside-outsider, because he spent most of his career in
General Electric's plastics business, considered peripheral within
GE. Boards can draw inside-outsiders from several places:

- A company's international division breeds inside-outsiders
  and tests leadership mettle in unfamiliar territory. International postings can expose managers to the world's best
  competitors before they hit the home market. Global
  competition also exposes managers to more sophisticated
  or more diverse customers than those of their domestic
  counterparts.

- Diversified business units at the periphery of the business
  are another great hunting ground. The combination of
  profit and loss responsibility with distance from headquarters creates promising grounds for experimentation with
  alternative success formulas.

- Inside-outsiders can be drawn from a company's lead bank.
  Jorma Ollila served as Nokia's loan officer at Citibank
  prior to joining the company and rising through the
  finance group. Hirotaro Higuchi joined Asahi Breweries
  from Sumitomo, the brewer's lead bank. Corporate

bankers often combine in-depth understanding of the company's business with a banker's disciplined perspective.

- Sometimes managers who leave a company and return later can serve as inside-outsiders. As a cofounder, Steve Jobs knows Apple intimately; however, his time away from the company allowed him to gain perspective before returning to turn it around.

Inside-outsiders offer a powerful solution to the dilemma of combining distance with knowledge. The power of inside-outsiders has different implications for board members, recently hired outsiders, inside senior executives, and middle managers.

External Board Members

Directors who worry that a company may be suffering from active inertia can begin to actively search out promising inside-outsiders prior to the point when crisis forces the board into a hasty decision. In evaluating promising candidates, directors can ask simply what these managers see as the company's key challenges going forward and how they would address them. Strong managers have often been stewing over these issues for months or years and can respond with a coherent (and often impassioned) analysis and set of recommendations. Most of the inside-outsiders that I have studied also spent some time in a prominent operating role in headquarters prior to becoming CEO. This trial period allows board members to assess whether the inside-outsider can avoid being too abrasive to get things done or, on the other hand, will go native and lose his passion to shake things up.

Outsiders

Recently hired executives can build teams that leverage the strengths of both insiders and outsiders. When Lou Gerstner took over as CEO of IBM in 1993, he didn't force out all of IBM's old guard. IBM veterans with decades of experience staffed many top operating positions. Gerstner complemented these insiders, however, with outside managers in critical staff roles—such as CFO and chief counsel—and marketing executives. The combination of inside and outside perspectives and experience allowed IBM to leverage its existing strengths in providing integrated solutions to customers while refreshing the company's brand and changing long-established operating processes.

Insiders

Veteran managers can, of course, adopt the mirror image approach to the strategy that they use by bringing outside managers into their inner circle. Insiders can also break free of their existing success formula by imagining what they would do if they were outsiders. Intel's top executives Andy Grove and Gordon Moore did exactly this when deciding to exit the memory business.[6-4] Intel had pioneered the market for memory chips, and its strategic frame that "Intel meant memory" had become a blinder that hindered managers from envisioning alternatives. As new competitors flooded the market with low-priced chips, however, Intel's share of the memory business shrank from over 90 percent in the early 1970s to about 5 percent in the 1980s. Increased competition not only eroded Intel's share, but also depressed memory chip prices and profits.

Intel had built a growing and profitable microprocessor business during this period. Top executives, however, continued to frame memory as the company's core business, despite mounting losses. Intel's then-president, Andy Grove, recounts how he and Chairman Gordon Moore deliberately visualized what would happen if the board replaced them with outside executives. Grove and Moore quickly concluded that outsiders would exit the memory business. Grove proposed that he and Moore walk out the door—figuratively speaking—return, and do themselves what outsiders would do if brought in by the board. Grove and Moore did exactly that and exited memory to focus on Intel's microprocessors.

Middle Managers

Midlevel managers in companies suffering from active inertia often throw up their hands in despair and complain that they can do nothing. Although transforming commitments indeed must come from the top of the company or a business unit, middle managers can contribute substantially to the effort. Like an outside board member, they can identify inside-outsiders within their firm who have the potential to lead the company. Middle managers can cultivate a relationship with these senior executives. They can also commit to transforming a business unit or subsidiary—provided they secure sufficient autonomy from top executives. Box 6-1 describes how middle managers within a large company led one successful transformation. Alternatively, they can prepare themselves for the day when a board member asks them what *they* see as the key challenges and how they would address them.

The Ethos of Commitments

In chapter 5, we discussed how managers must select a transformational commitment—a new strategic direction, resource base, process, stretch relationship, or set of values—that fits the company's circumstances. Alignment between the anchor and the context is necessary but not sufficient for the transformation to succeed. The most effective transforming commitments are also consistent with the *ethos*—or personal values and past actions—of the manager making the commitment.

A disconnect between *what* a manager commits to and *who* he is can be disastrous. I witnessed this firsthand while facilitating a leadership development program for a technology company lost

BOX 6-1

Transforming Commitments in the Middle

MIDDLE MANAGERS CAN sometimes transform divisions within a larger corporation, even if the company as a whole remains trapped in active inertia. The successful transformation of Shell's retail gasoline operations in Hungary illustrates how middle managers can lead the charge.[5] Royal Dutch/Shell's corporate financial performance lagged its competitors throughout the early 1990s, which prompted Chairman Cornelius Herkstroter to commit to doubling the group's profits between 1997 and 2001. He also pledged to close or sell any business that fell short of corporate performance goals.

The new financial targets certainly awakened the management of Shell's retail chain of 115 gasoline stations in Hungary. Although it was the most profitable gasoline retailer in Hungary, Shell still returned less than one-third the required level on average capital employed. Shell's local management—led by the chairman of Shell Hungary, George Mosonyi, and sales manager Istvan Kapitany—committed to increasing nonfuel revenues from the Shell Select gas stations with convenience stores. Items like candy bars, sandwiches, and sodas netted higher margins than gasoline. The Hungarian convenience food market, moreover, was highly fragmented relative to Western Europe countries, enabling Shell to seize market share.

Mosonyi and Kapitany took several actions to fulfill their commitment to nonfuel retail. They redefined the job of the account managers of the stores, recasting "rent collectors" who worried about pumping gas and taking cash into "mini-CEOs" who could decide for themselves what to sell and what prices to charge. In the past, Shell had forced managers to comply with precisely detailed layouts of products stocked and sold in the shop. Shell penalized local managers for deviating from these store maps—called "planograms"—even for moving chocolate bars out of direct sunlight to prevent melting. Mosonyi and Kapitany encouraged local managers to experiment with the product mix, allowed them to hire and fire staff, held them accountable for profit and loss, and tied bonuses to their business performance.

The results of these actions were dramatic. Shell nonfuel retail sales grew significantly, increasing 60 percent in 1991. Shell touts its Hungarian retail operations as a glowing success story. Kapitany was voted the best manager in Hungary, and the Hungarian national oil company wooed Mosonyi away. The success of Shell Hungary's transformation illustrates the more general conditions that increase the middle manager's odds of successful transformation.

- **The manager has sufficient autonomy to make the transforming commitment.** This requires sufficient distance from headquarters to avoid interference from top executives steeped in the existing success formula. Shell was noted for the independence of its national businesses.

- **The manager's commitment is consistent with broader corporate direction.** Shell Hungary's shift to nonfuel sales was consistent with the chairman's goal of doubling profits in five years. In fact, it provided a model that other divisions later emulated.

- **The manager can obtain sufficient capital to finance the transformation.** Transformations generally cost money, and managers need the capital without corporate interference that might derail the effort. The Shell transformation required little incremental capital, so Shell Hungary's top management team could fund it on their own dime.

- **The manager can credibly pledge to stay long enough to fulfill the commitment.** When subordinates believe that their division is a manager's rest-stop en route to the executive suite, they often wait on the sidelines until he moves to the next job. Since both Mosonyi and Kapitany were Hungarian, employees expected them to stay long enough to deal with the consequences of their actions.

amid the industry turbulence. The session culminated in a discussion with the newly appointed president, who had risen through the ranks of the company's engineering division. A participant asked the new president about his vision for the company's future. The room went silent. The president paused, opened his briefcase, and flatly read a statement of the company's commitment to speed in new product launches. The audience deflated like a pricked balloon.

In the debriefing, many participants agreed that a commitment to speeding the new product development process could serve as the anchor for pulling the company from active inertia. The managers *unanimously* agreed, however, that the new president was *not* the person to push for speed. They doubted whether this man, renowned for his methodical (some said plodding) attention to detail, could personally forgo the elaborate checkpoints in new product development to gain speed, even if he understood intellectually that the company needed to do it. Their skepticism was borne out. The new president would not dismantle the company's existing processes, and the company continued to introduce products more slowly than its rivals. His tenure was short.

Successful managers, in contrast, exhibit a close alignment between what they commit to and who they are. Marvin Bower's commitment to professional values rang true because he had been trained as a lawyer and personally embodied the values that he infused in McKinsey. Lou Gerstner's standing as a former IBM customer lent credibility to his pledge to solve customers' problems. Consistency between a manager's ethos and her commitments not only provides credibility, it also increases the likelihood that she will consistently "walk the talk."

Matching ethos and public commitments also helps managers communicate more effectively and persuasively. This observation is not new. In fact, we can trace its origins to the ancient study of rhetoric.[6] The term *rhetoric* has fallen into disrepute in modern times, serving as a foil to something worthwhile—"rhetoric versus reality" or "rhetoric versus action." Classical authors, however, defined rhetoric as the art of persuading people to act.[7] Aristotle argued that the most effective rhetoric derives its power from three sources: *logos*, which convinces rationally; *pathos*, which touches the listeners' emotions; and *ethos*, which builds on the speaker's personal credibility. While managers can rely exclusively on one mode, the most effective speakers combine all three elements to convey their commitment.

The rhetoric of Jack Welch illustrates the logos-pathos-ethos framework perfectly. Although many authors have explored *what* Welch said—themes such as number 1 or number 2, borderless organization, or Work Out—few have analyzed *how* he said it. As a result, managers who try to transplant Welch's ideas into their own company find that they fail to take root. In my assessment, it was not the novelty of Welch's ideas that explain their power but his brilliance at drawing on all three elements of rhetoric to communicate them to tens of thousands of employees.

How did Welch use logos? Logos consists of fact-based logical arguments that convince the listeners intellectually. Strategic consultants—and managers drawn from their ranks—are exemplary practitioners of this mode. Rhetoric based on logos need not be complicated to be effective. The most persuasive ideas are often the simplest (but not the most simple-minded). One recurrent theme in Jack Welch's rhetoric at General Electric, for example, was the "need for speed." Welch did not construct elaborate deductive arguments to support his position, but rather outlined—and quantified—the advantages of speed. He related, for example, how shortening the time between customer orders and delivery helped GE boost inventory turns from less than five in the mid-1980s to nearly eight by 1997. Every single-digit improvement in inventory turns, he explained, freed $1 billion in cash. These uncomplicated illustrations succeeded by appealing to the audience's intellect.

Welch went on to touch listeners' emotions. One important element of GE's transformation under Welch was "Work Out," a series of assemblies that brought together large cross-sections of a business unit to identify ways to dismantle bureaucracy. Work Out struck at the core of middle managers' authority, and many initially resisted the meetings. To win middle managers over, Welch relied not only on logical arguments, but also on evocative stories. Once, he related the anecdote of a tough union leader who historically had three clearly defined enemies: the Internal Revenue Service, the Russians, and GE's management. After the fall of the Berlin Wall and GE's introduction of Work Out, Welch said, this unlikely ally conceded that he had only the IRS left to hate.

Managers can increase the emotional appeal of their messages by painting vivid verbal pictures that support their point, a tactic that classical authors termed *enargeia*. Welch used a series of images to evoke the evils of bureaucracy. He likened managers padded by excessive reporting layers to someone clad in several sweaters on a winter day: "They remain warm and comfortable but are blissfully ignorant of the realities of their environment." He derided bureaucratic documents as "something out of the National Archives, with five, ten, or even more signatures required before action can be taken." To emphasize the resilience of bad habits, Welch talked about the "dandelions of bureaucracy . . . that don't come up easily and will be back next week if you don't keep after them." He characterized bureaucracy as the "Dracula of institutional behavior, that will rise and rise again." Welch's memorable stories and images reinforced his ideas.

Although logos and pathos deliver a powerful punch, a third component is necessary for rhetoric to achieve its full potential. Ethos—a leader's personal character—is crucial to building the credibility and trust necessary to persuade. Listeners can quickly discern whether a speaker's rhetoric fits with his personal identity. Welch exuded a fierce competitive spirit, honed in the hockey rinks of his youth, that authenticated his message of speed, simplicity, and self-confidence. Even some of his ideas and imagery—layers of sweaters, New England town meetings—arose from his Massachusetts upbringing. Based on his word choice, anyone who heard him could tell that he drew from his own experience, rather than from the pages of the latest management tome. This alignment greatly enhanced his rhetoric (see figure 6-1).

FIGURE 6-1

The Rhetoric of Commitment

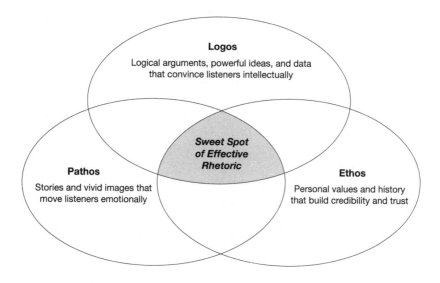

On the other hand, misalignment of character and commitment—like espousing one set of values publicly, then promoting a highly successful subordinate who blatantly flouts those values—can instantly shatter a leader's credibility. Nor can excellence in logos and pathos compensate for shortcomings in ethos, as Bill Clinton's presidency illustrates. Few presidents combined Clinton's mastery of technical detail with his gift for touching people's emotions. But inconsistencies between his commitments and actions sharply curtailed the persuasiveness of his rhetoric. Ethos is fragile, like an eggshell; once you break the bond between character and words, you can never restore it to its former quality. Box 6-2, Rhetoric in Action, provides concrete advice for improving your rhetoric.

Selecting the right person to lead the charge is critical, but breaking out of active inertia is by no means a solo activity. It is very much a team sport. Actually, transformation requires several

BOX 6-2

Rhetoric in Action

GREAT COMMUNICATORS are made, not born, said the classical authors. They believed that leaders could remake themselves into compelling speakers by using the following techniques.

Declare a Crisis

The starting point for every rhetorical opportunity is an exigence, "an imperfection marked by urgency," according to the philosopher Lloyd Bitzer. "It is a defect, an obstacle, something waiting to be done, a thing that is other than it should be."[8] The exigence creates an imbalance that cries out for resolution and thereby invites action. A manager can wait until a company approaches the brink of bankruptcy and then declare a crisis. By this point, however, the company often lacks the resources and alternatives needed to move forward. The trick is declaring an exigence before the situation deteriorates too far. Here are some common tactics.

Redefine Success

Rather than waiting for performance to deteriorate, managers can reframe what constitutes acceptable performance. Jack Welch, for example, became CEO in 1981 as GE experienced record sales and profits. Welch redefined success by declaring that every business in the GE portfolio must be number 1 or number 2 in its market. The number 1 or number 2 mantra created urgency where none had existed before. It shifted managers' attention away from GE's short-term financial performance, which had not yet registered the company's competitive erosion in the late 1970s. Compared to the best global competitors, many GE businesses were poorly positioned. Realization of this gap created a new and urgent problem that required action.

Seize a Short-Term Crisis to Solve a Long-Term Problem

Managers can harness the urgency from a short-term problem to push through more sweeping reforms. Masashi Kaneko ascended to the CEO position at Nikko Securities during a corporate racketeering scandal. Although Kaneko expected to sort out the racketeering-related problems within a year, he used the crisis to make changes that would help Nikko solve its longer-term challenge of competing with global firms entering the newly opened Japanese market. The Japanese word for crisis—kiki—consists of two characters. One, "ki," means threat; the other means opportunity. Managers can use the opportunity portion of a crisis to create the need for action.

The Devil Made Me Do It

An exigence has more power when the target audience believes external events have forced the issue. Such external triggers include rumored hostile takeovers, a sharp drop in market share or stock price, or even a report by external consultants.

Broaden Your Scope

The most powerful rhetoric combines logos, pathos, and ethos. Most leaders, however, rely heavily or exclusively on their strongest style, when they could communicate their commitment with more power by diversifying to include other styles. A manager who generally favors logical analysis, for example, will get more marginal impact from a well-chosen story than from the incremental PowerPoint exhibit. A few simple questions can help you diversify your rhetoric.

Logos

In articulating the exigence requiring action, can you provide incontrovertible data? Can you quantify the benefits of action? Can you argue clearly and convincingly for your chosen commitment? Did you consider alternatives? Why did you reject them? The key to success in this stage is the move beyond opinion and assertion to fact-based analysis and clear ideas.

Pathos

You can actively hunt for stories within your company that illustrate why transformation is necessary or how you plan to change things. What story best illustrates your point? What emotions did the story evoke for you? What emotions does it evoke in listeners? In retelling the story, do you personally feel inspired? Do listeners respond the same way? Imagine that a group of middle managers asks you for a concrete example of your commitment; how would you reply?

Ethos

You can check ethos by examining whether your transforming commitments resonate with your own experience. Can you remember the exact moment when the need for change dawned on you? When the right anchor crystallized in your mind? Can you draw on your previous experience to explain why you are the right person for the commitment?

different teams. Managers who understand how these teams work will more likely harness their cumulative power.

Basketball Team

A manager's direct reports most closely resemble a basketball team. The top management team generally consists of a handful of people (usually four to six), who divide up their roles and spend a lot of time on the court together. Managers must first ensure that all members of the core team are on board. When Jorma Ollila was appointed CEO of Nokia, for example, he quickly staffed key positions with a group of young Turks (young Finns, actually), who understood Nokia's need for transformation and bought into Ollila's commitment to telecommunications.

Doubles Tennis

Sometimes a duo can lead a successful transformation effort. Pairing a bold thinker with a disciplined doer can assure both an unconventional vision and unflinching execution. Lloyds TSB chairman, the visionary Jeremy Morse, argued that English bankers should focus on their profitable domestic business rather than squander resources on diversification and globalization. Translating this insight into action, his colleague Brian Pitman led Lloyds TSB's exit from its unprofitable diversified enterprises.

Pit Crews

Managers can treat their relationships with advisors, including management consultants, investment bankers, and lawyers, like a Formula One driver's partnership with his pit crew. The leader works with them periodically to solve specific problems. But no one should ever mistake the pit crew for the driver.

Tag-Team Wrestling

Some managers think that they must reverse all their predecessor's commitments to distance themselves from the past. Earlier managers, however, often lay much of the groundwork necessary for later success. The incremental changes to Asahi Breweries' new product development process made by Higuchi's predecessor, Tsutomu Murai, generated a series of new products, including Asahi Draft and Asahi Dry. Thus, Murai's earlier actions produced the alternative to which his successor could commit. Ollila's predecessor at Nokia protected the telecommunications division despite early losses, and this business provided the cornerstone of Nokia's later transformation.

Successful transformation, you will recall, often results when a leader throws her weight behind an alternative that already existed within a company. The last generation of managers is often the one that generated and protected the foundation for the later transformation, even if as individuals they lacked the energy, insight, or courage to commit fully to the new future. New managers should, at minimum, understand what value their predecessors created to avoid throwing out the baby with the bathwater. Ideally, they should acknowledge the debt to their predecessors. The transformational leader will get credit for the goal; she should at least grant that her predecessors provided the assist.

The Right Deal

Any manager considering a major transformation should first ask himself a few key questions. We have covered some of these already: Which anchor does my organization need most? Am I the right person for the job? Can I assemble the right team to support me? The deal between the manager and the boss raises an additional set of questions. At the corporate level, the agreement between the CEO and the board of directors constitutes this deal. At a business-unit level, the agreement occurs between the division president and the top executives. Following are a few questions that you should discuss.

How Much Support Will I Have?

Transforming a company's success formula demands tough calls. You may need to exit legacy businesses or challenge long-held frames and operating procedures. Before leading the charge, managers should gauge their level of support for change. At the corporate level, the CEO should ask: Who are the influential directors and constituencies (e.g., founding family representatives, major investors)? How do they view the situation? Can they stomach difficult decisions? Divisional managers should ask themselves a similar set of questions about their company's top management team.

How Much Time Do I Have?

Breaking free of active inertia takes time. Too short a tenure carries two risks. First, the board or top management team may declare defeat prematurely and pull the plug before the results are clear. Second, subordinates may abstain from change if they believe that they can simply wait it out. In the Pentagon, for example, career bureaucrats know that they can outlast any political appointees who might push for change. A similar pattern plays out in large companies that regularly rotate middle managers. A new manager comes to head a business unit but receives only lip service from the division's veterans, who fully expect (rightly in these cases) the high-flying executive to leave before any real change takes place.

How Will I Be Compensated?

Executives have come under fire recently for compensation packages deemed outrageous. In some cases, these packages were, in fact, scandalous. Managers attempting to transform an existing organization, however, take on a very risky job. The payoff for success can be high—Nokia, IBM, and Samsung, for example, created tremendous shareholder value. But the odds of failure are high.

In many ways, the payoffs for leading a transformation are even riskier than those of starting a new venture. In both cases, the odds of failure are high. Most people understand that a start-up venture can very easily fail and they admire the entrepreneur's courage; thus entrepreneurs usually avoid the stigma of failure, even if their new venture never actually makes or sells anything. Indeed, venture capitalists and headhunters sometimes deem failed entrepreneurs more valuable for their real-world experience.

Failures on the résumé are like battle scars and war medals; they show that entrepreneurs have seen real action and survived to try again. In contrast, the press often derides managers who failed to transform an existing organization; indeed, these managers often struggle to find another challenging position. Even if they succeed, their financial gains may be criticized as "outsized" in a way that entrepreneurs' wealth rarely is.

So that managers will bear the risk of transformation, they should receive a compensation package that provides them a share of the upside (through options or equity) if business goes well, as well as a severance package that, if the transformation fails, compensates them for the downside (a risk to their future earning potential). Admittedly, such a compensation package may not suit every situation—like that of an executive expected simply to stabilize a company. The prevalence of such packages may partly reflect the increased need for transformation in a more uncertain world.

———

This chapter provides guidance on selecting the right person to make the transforming commitments. Chapter 7 describes how managers can make their commitments more effective.

SEVEN

Giving Your
Commitments Traction

IN THE PRECEDING CHAPTERS, we discussed selecting the right anchor for your organization and picking the right person for the job. As arduous and intense as this preparation might have been, the hard labor lies ahead. Once you choose an anchor, you either use it or lose it. This chapter provides guidance on motivating people to understand and accept your commitments and modify their own behavior accordingly.[1]

Think of the ice climbers. After selecting the belay anchor, the leader must secure it firmly before pulling the other climbers up. Similarly, a manager must secure the chosen anchor—no simple task, because her company's historical blinders, millstones, routines, shackles, and dogmas tend to drag the organization back into the status quo. The manager must drive this anchor deeply to use it as a lever for the rest of the organization. The greater the weight of past commitments, the more secure the anchor must be.

My research suggests that effective transforming commitments share three characteristics. They are credible, clear, and courageous, or what I call the "Three Cs" of effective commitments. The story of Lars Kolind's transformation of the Danish hearing aid maker Oticon shows these traits in action.

Think the Unthinkable: The Oticon Story

The Danish hearing-aid maker Oticon is a classic case of a good company gone bad.[2] For decades, Oticon led the global market in hearing aids, exporting 90 percent of its production. Then, in the 1980s, a rival introduced the first in-the-ear hearing aid, a device less conspicuous than Oticon's behind-the-ear models. Convenient and cosmetically appealing, the in-the-ear devices rapidly gained popularity—particularly after then-president Ronald Reagan started wearing one. But Oticon's engineers firmly believed in their traditional product's superior sound quality. They responded to the new technology by doing more of the same, producing and selling highly engineered behind-the-ear products through traditional distribution channels. Locked in active inertia, Oticon lost half its global market share.

In the late 1980s, the board turned outside for a new CEO and tapped Lars Kolind, who had built the third-largest consulting firm in Denmark, run the country's National Science Research Laboratory, and served as a leader in the global Boy Scouts. Kolind stanched Oticon's bleeding by cutting 15 percent of the workforce and consolidating budget approval authority from seventy-eight people to one—he personally signed every check. After saving the company from bankruptcy, Kolind surveyed the competitive landscape. The picture was bleak. The company had lost its market share and its technical lead to well-financed competitors. Siemens alone invested more in R&D of hearing-related technology than Oticon booked in annual revenues. Kolind concluded that Oticon's only alternative lay in out-innovating its larger competitors—specifically by developing and marketing new products more quickly.

Kolind selected Oticon's new product development process to anchor the transformation.[3] At the time, Oticon was organized into functional fiefdoms; R&D tossed elegant designs over to manufacturing, which tossed the finished product over to the sales force. Kolind committed to a new process in which cross-functional teams would assemble to develop a new product, collaborate for the duration of a project, and then disband. Anyone could propose and pursue a new project if she garnered support from three parties: a management champion, the top executive team for funding, and employees to staff the team. Any of the three participants could kill a project by withdrawing support.

Kolind kicked off his transformation with a memo, headed "Thinking the Unthinkable," that outlined his vision of and argument for the new process. Unlike many managers, however, Kolind recognized that one memo does not an effective transformation make. Determined to "drop a nuclear bomb" (his words) on Oticon's bureaucracy, he spent two months telling employees and middle managers that he was 100 percent committed to this change—and that they would have to commit, too, or leave the company altogether. Kolind's commitment made boosters of everyone but the middle managers, whose status was at risk. Kolind enlisted some of the resistant managers to plan the transition and encouraged the others to leave.

Kolind's subsequent bold actions demonstrated he was serious. He publicly auctioned off Oticon's old hardwood furniture and used the proceeds to purchase desks, chairs, and cabinets on wheels so that employees could roll their desks and files from one team to another. In August 1991, Kolind invited the Danish press to televise Oticon's move to its new headquarters, an abandoned Tuborg beer factory with an enormous work space and no enclosed offices. Under such press scrutiny, Oticon staff felt compelled to make the transformation work. Finally, Kolind acquired 17 percent of Oticon's stock with his own savings.

The new process served Oticon remarkably well throughout the 1990s. Project-based development produced the world's first microprocessor-based hearing aid that automatically adjusts sounds to the users' hearing range. Oticon reemerged as a technical leader in the hearing aid market, winning the European Design Prize in 1996, cutting time to market by nearly 50 percent, and increasing revenues threefold between 1990 and 1998.

The Three Cs of Effective Commitments

The Oticon story illustrates how managers *give their transforming commitments traction.* Kolind's commitments were credible because of his conspicuous public steps and financial investment. Kolind's anchor was clear, never straying from his first vivid memorandum. Finally, his actions were courageous, all clean breaks from Oticon's bureaucratic past. How can you apply the three Cs to your own transformation? The following three sections (summarized in figure 7-1) explain.

Be Credible

A manager's commitments are credible to the extent that other people believe she will stay the course even when changes in the business context might promote another course of action in the future.[4] If customers, employees, colleagues, partners, or other stakeholders believe that the manager will be steadfast in honoring her commitment, then they will adjust their own behavior accordingly. For example, if employees trust the manager's commitment to achieving six-sigma quality, then they will work harder to achieve six-sigma in their own division. Employees' actions, in turn, increase the odds of success, giving credibility. The additional effort further enhances credibility and attracts the remaining fence-sitters. A self-fulfilling prophesy begins.

FIGURE 7-1

The Three Cs of Effective Transforming Commitments

Credible
Have you made hard-to-reverse investments?

Have you burned your bridges behind you?

Have you staked your personal reputation?

Have you staked your company's reputation?

Have you put your money where your mouth is?

Have you put your best people where your mouth is?

Have you put your time where your mouth is?

Have you handed over the keys?

Clear
Is your commitment simple?

Is your commitment concrete?

Can you measure progress?

   Can you quantify the measure?

   How frequently will you measure?

   When do you select the measure?

   Who will measure progress? Inside the company? Outside the company?

Have you repeated your commitment often enough?

   Are you sick of repeating it? Are others?

   Could employees pass a pop quiz?

Courageous
Are you breaking from the pack?

Are you ignoring the "experts"?

Is this a quantum leap or an incremental change?

Are you hedging your bets or covering your backside?

Are you undoing your predecessor's actions?

Could you do it faster or sooner?

Recall Asahi Breweries, where Hirotaro Higuchi's investment in new capacity and advertising, in addition to yanking old beer off the shelves, virtually eliminated the brewer's ability to pursue alternatives. Employees realized that the company had few options if the dry beer failed, and so they had to make dry beer work. Asahi's large investment also convinced skeptical distributors of Asahi's resolve to make Asahi Dry a success, despite the company's habit of launching products without sufficient marketing and sales follow-up. Convinced of Asahi's resolution, distributors allocated more shelf space to the new beer, thereby increasing its odds of success. The large investment may even have deterred competitors, since Asahi's capacity exceeded the known level of dry beer demand.[5]

Of course, establishing a commitment's credibility does not guarantee a successful transformation. The Asahi story would have ended in tears if demand for dry beer had proved to be a passing fad. That said, credibility does matter when success depends on the behavior of customers, employees, distributors, and competitors who can observe and respond to a manager's public actions. When success does depend on stakeholders reconciling their actions with the chosen direction, then the manager must create occasions to "walk the talk"—to demonstrate his commitment. Managers can use the following questions to assess whether they have made their commitment credible.

Have you made hard-to-reverse investments?   Managers can increase the credibility of their transforming commitments by irreversibly locking their organization into a specific course of action. Had dry beer floundered, Asahi could not have recovered the large investment in advertising nor transferred it back to the company's lager. When Chuck Pilliod took over Goodyear, he invested every dollar he could get his hands on for new capacity. Had radials misfired or foreign competitors dominated the market, Goodyear shareholders would have owned a chain of very expensive covered parking garages (a.k.a. useless tire factories).

Have you burned your bridges behind you?   Managers can also strengthen credibility by closing off the past. When Jorma Ollila committed Nokia to the telecommunications market, he sold off the other businesses. Had mobile phones flopped, Nokia could not have reverted to smoothing its earnings across diversified businesses. When Lars Kolind sold Oticon's traditional headquarters and auctioned off the old furniture, he barred middle managers from hiding behind solid oak desks with their office doors shut.

Have you staked your reputation publicly?   Managers need not invest money to buy credibility; they can stake their reputation. The more public a commitment, the more damaging a retraction to the manager's personal credibility. Managers must announce their commitments to both external and internal communities. Within months of becoming chairman, Lee Kun-Hee, for example, publicly declared to employees that Samsung required a "Second Foundation" and later declared his independence from the Korean government. Lars Kolind took public commitment to a new level when he invited the Danish press to cover Oticon's move.

Have you put your money where your mouth is?   Managers can increase credibility by linking compensation to hitting the targets. Lars Kolind, for example, acquired 17 percent of Oticon before making his transformational commitment. Brian Pitman of Lloyds TSB pioneered a companywide system for tying compensation to increases in shareholder value. How much skin in the game do you personally have? What will you gain if all goes well? What do you forfeit if all goes south? In assessing whether a manager's commitments are for real, employees and others often invoke Jerry Maguire's tagline—"show me the money."

Have you put your best people where your mouth is?   Managers send strong signals through personnel decisions. Have you removed any key managers from profitable businesses to support your transformation? If a senior manager hits his numbers but does so by using the old success formula and undermining your commitments, do you promote, hold, or demote him? Will you remove people who thrived under the status quo but wilt under the new demands? Will you hire people with more knowledge and expertise than you have? Will you give them what they need— namely, the autonomy and the resources—to do what you hired them to do?

Many managers flinch when they recognize the tough people decisions that they must make. But employees see this hesitation and assess credibility based on how a manager handles these tough personnel calls.

Have you put your time where your mouth is?　Managers' allocation of time sends a powerful signal about their priorities. Recall how Gerstner shocked his subordinates by spending a few days rather than a few hours with leading customers. One CEO invited the quality guru W. Edwards Deming to explain TQM (total quality management) to his top managers. He escorted Deming to the conference room, introduced Deming, then left. As he walked down the hallway, he heard shuffling noises behind him. He turned—and found Deming behind him. "If it's not important enough for you to be there," Deming told him, "Then it's not important for me to be there either." How many hours per week are you spending on making your transforming commitments work?

Have you handed over the keys?　Managers can enhance credibility by surrendering rights over critical decisions to outside stakeholders. This approach works particularly well with vows to stretch relationships. Recall how Nikko Securities sold a 20 percent stake to Salomon Smith Barney to cement the deal. Nikko management also ceded key decision rights to the joint venture. These actions increased the chances that Nikko would change because the agreement made it harder for either partner to walk. Franck Riboud, to cite another example, voluntarily listed shares of the French food company Danone on the New York Stock Exchange at a time when many other European executives were scurrying to avoid capital market interference. By voluntarily listing on the NYSE, Riboud not only gained access to capital but also tapped into pressure to increase shareholder value and harnessed that tension to drive change throughout Danone. At the same time, he exposed himself and his company to investor intervention, which authenticated Riboud's commitment to shareholders.

Be Clear

Successful transforming commitments share the virtue of clarity. Recall Lou Gerstner's commitment to provide integrated solutions, Jack Welch's insistence on being number 1 or number 2, Jorma Ollila's bet on global telecommunications, Brian Pitman's commitment to shareholders, or Hirotaro Higuchi's push for dry beer. In each case, employees or investors might agree or disagree with the commitment or, indeed, the need for transformation. Everyone understood, however, what the manager was saying.

Clarity is not a coincidence but a necessary condition for three reasons. First, clarity increases credibility.[6] External parties can measure and verify progress toward a clearly articulated commitment; that is, they can see whether a manager is walking the talk. Ambiguous or vague commitments leave so much wriggle room that people dismiss them as irrelevant. Second, clear commitments are easier to communicate within an organization and to outside stakeholders. Communicating throughout a large and complex organization is like a children's game of telephone, where the first child whispers the designated phrase to the child next to her, who repeats the phrase to the next child, and so on around the circle. Vague, long, or complicated messages get garbled in the transmission, whereas crisp, clear ones pass with fewer distortions. Finally, clear commitments provide an easy-to-visualize alternative to the status quo. Employees will more likely kick organizational habits if they can imagine the alternative anchor. The following questions can help assess the clarity of your commitments.

Is your commitment simple?   Articulating a simple commitment forces a manager to work the problem until she can distill it to its essence. This distillation can help managers to grasp the organization's challenges more firmly and choose the best commitment for their situation. In contrast, complex commitments generally result from cursory preparation. One management team, for example, committed to "serving our customers with integrity and making quality the cornerstone of our business while providing our employees with opportunities for personal development and creating value for our owners in a socially responsible manner." That statement is not a commitment; it's a laundry list. Simple commitments entail an implicit prioritization that focuses attention.

Effective anchors tend to be simple. That doesn't imply that all simple anchors are effective. One of the greatest dangers is to seize upon a simple formula before wrestling with the full complexity of your specific situation. Managers do this when they mindlessly adopt off-the-shelf solutions. Management buzzwords may be simple, but they do not guarantee a fit with you or your organization. "I would not give a fig for the simplicity this side of complexity," Oliver Wendell Holmes observed, "but would give my life for the simplicity on the other side of complexity."[7]

You can apply a few quick tests to see whether your commitment is simple enough. Can you articulate it from memory? If you fail this test, then you have a serious problem. Can anyone else in the organization—particularly front-line employees—articulate it from memory? Can you boil it down to a "phrase that pays" of five words or fewer? Failing any of these tests suggests that you should grapple more with complexity to arrive at a simple commitment.

Is your commitment concrete?   An anchor can be simple and still be too vague to provide much guidance. Broad concepts such as "value," "achievement," "flexibility," "entrepreneurship," "innovation," "empowerment," "integrity," and "respect" are too intangible. None of these notions is bad, per se, but these concepts raise more questions than they answer about expected behavior. Contrast these foggy notions with the concreteness of leadership in radial technology or owned distribution at Pepsi. The difference is not simplicity but specificity.

Can you give three concrete examples of actions, such as investments, disinvestments, public promises, and so on that would be consistent with your direction? On the other side, can you give three examples of attractive opportunities that your company should pass by? Pose these same questions to other employees in your organization and see if you agree with their examples.

Can you measure progress?   Measuring progress can directly refocus an organization in a new direction. Transforming commitments vary in the ease with which progress can be measured. Process improvement and a new strategic direction are easier to measure than shifts in stretch relationships and values. Companies have, however, come up with innovative ways to measure progress toward even the softest of commitments. The following questions help assess whether you can measure progress, while the examples may spark some ideas on how to measure it.

CAN YOU QUANTIFY THE MEASURE?   The quantification test often roots out vague or ambiguous commitments. Try quantifying "empowerment" or "flexibility." Part of the appeal of process improvement programs like TQM or six-sigma as anchors results from their strict quantification of defect rates. Stretch relationships can also be quantified. A Brazilian textiles manufacturer, for example, committed to a stretch relationship by severing its ties to wholesalers and selling directly to sophisticated U.S. clothing manufacturers. The owner measured success by the percentage of sales to U.S. clothing companies and by customer satisfaction data, which she collected twice per year. By carefully tracking revenues from consulting fees and sales commissions, an English insurance broker measured progress in moving from underwriting to advising clients.

One of the reasons commitments to new values rarely succeed is the difficulty of quantifying progress, but even here it's possible. Pepsi-Cola managers, for example, articulated a set of values, interviewed managers and employees to develop concrete examples of behavior consistent and inconsistent with these values, then surveyed employees annually on their managers' conformance to these values and the associated behavior.

HOW FREQUENTLY WILL YOU MEASURE?   The timing of measurement contributes both to the sense of urgency associated with transforming commitments and to their credibility. Compaq's Eckhard Pfeiffer, for example, set the goal of becoming the number 1 PC maker by 1996 and overtook IBM to achieve that goal on schedule. An open pledge to become the market leader at some indefinite point in the future, in contrast, would have sapped Pfeiffer's goal of its urgency.

WHEN DO YOU SELECT THE MEASURE?   You might think that the first thing to do when starting to transform a company is set a clear measure. There are advantages, however, to waiting. After committing to shareholders' interests, Brian Pitman worked with his top management team and board to select the best metric. They first tried return on capital, then returns relative to peer banks, before settling on the formula of doubling market value every three years. Working through alternative measures helped Pitman educate his team and board on what a commitment to shareholders would mean in practice. The time also allowed him to experiment with alternative metrics until he hit on a measure that embodied continuous improvement. As long as each of the metrics measures progress toward the same anchor, changing them over time will not derail the transformation.

WHO WILL MEASURE?   Third-party measurement is more credible than internal measurement. Duck-Yang managers, for example, called on their largest customer, Hyundai, and an external quality institute to monitor their reductions in product defects. The manager of a European trading firm committed to a stretch relationship with central banks in emerging markets, rather than the firm's traditional corporate clients. Management measured not only the percentage of revenues generated from the central banks, but also the firm's standing in the league tables published by industry trade journals like *Euromoney*.

Have you repeated your commitment often enough?   Constant repetition has the obvious benefits of forcing you to distill your commitment down to its quintessence and to reinforce the message. Managers often err when they state their commitment once or twice, maybe send out a memo or two, and then assume that the rest of the organization will act on it. In large, geographically dispersed organizations, employees are deluged with messages from above. Some of these conflict with one another. Others prove to be passing fads. Mentioning a commitment a few times is the organizational equivalent of a teenager mumbling. You may know what you said, but no one else will. Here are a few simple tests to evaluate whether you are repeating your anchor consistently enough.

ARE YOU SICK OF REPEATING IT?   If not, then you must say it more often. Even if you can no longer stand your message, you must keep repeating it, so as not to miss that new employee or the person just back from maternity leave.

DO YOUR MANAGERS ROLL THEIR EYES WHEN YOU REPEAT YOUR MESSAGE?   Eye-rolling is a good sign—it shows that they already recognize your theme.

WOULD ANYONE IN YOUR COMPANY PASS A POP QUIZ? After a month or so, ask your direct reports to write your commitment on a single stick-on note. How many could do so? How many of their direct reports could pass the quiz as well? What if you administered the same test to equity analysts, key customers, partners, and your board members?

Be Courageous

Managers often respond to active inertia by acting incrementally, thereby reinforcing the status quo. This response is not always wrong. Recall that transforming commitments do not suit every company. If you can sustain your current position and you lack better alternatives, then reinforcing commitments will do no harm. However, if you (or those in the executive suite) have already decided that your company's survival depends on transforming commitments, then you will require courage. Transforming commitments are daring to the extent that they break with the existing formula rather than fortify it. The following questions can help you calibrate the audacity of your transforming commitments.

Are you breaking from the pack?   The extent to which your transforming commitments differ from those of your peers provides one measure of courage. Other Japanese brewers considered Higuchi's decision to push a nonlager beer as somewhere between desperate and foolhardy. Brian Pitman's commitment to increasing shareholder value led him to increase his focus on domestic retail financial services when England's other High Street banks were diversifying out of retail banking. While Samsung committed to building its technology and brand, the other large competitors continued to rely on quantity and government support.

Are you ignoring the "experts"?   Equity analysts, journalists, and industry experts are generally suspicious of transforming commitments. Many computer industry experts believed that Lou Gerstner should dismember IBM into Baby Blues. Experts are not always wrong and managers are not always right. Still, managers must have the courage of their convictions. Raising a company from its active inertia requires a leadership compass, not a weather vane that shifts course with every passing breeze.

Is this move a quantum leap or a toe in the water?   When Asahi's engineers proposed a 30 percent increase in dry beer capacity as the most aggressive possibility, Higuchi demanded 50 percent to force them outside the box. Quantum changes are not revolutions. Managers *should not attempt* wholesale change all at once and *should not demand* radical change for its own sake. Rather, they should demand nonincremental change in the areas required to fulfill their commitments.

Are you hedging your bets or covering your backside? Transforming commitments are inherently risky, and only a reckless manager would ignore these risks or fail to manage them.

Nokia's Ollila bet the company on telecommunications, but he maintained flexibility by remaining agnostic on technical standards. Managers must answer honestly: "Do we need this flexibility because we face genuine uncertainty or am I simply shying away from doing what we must do?" Duck-Yang's managers, for example, considered and ultimately rejected the option of beginning their process improvement on a peripheral product line. They decided instead to begin with their major product, reasoning that they could not afford the cost of delay and the lost urgency.

Are you undoing your predecessor's actions? Managers sometimes avoid reversing their predecessors' decisions, particularly if these executives mentored them or drove the company's historical success. Danone's Franck Riboud, for example, succeeded his father, who had grown the business through successive high-profile acquisitions. Rather than acquire like Riboud *père*, Riboud *fils* committed to a new strategic frame: Danone would achieve maximum revenues with minimum product lines. To meet this commitment, Riboud *fils* divested several of the businesses that his *père* had acquired.

Could you do it faster or sooner? Even the most successful managers regret not making their transforming commitments sooner. Jack Welch, whose early nickname, Neutron Jack, hardly suggests a wilting lily, expressed his regret over not acting bolder and faster. Welch can admit it. Can you?

––––––––––––

This chapter introduced the three Cs model to help managers give their transforming commitments traction. Chapter 8 discusses some common mistakes to dodge while leading a transformation.

EIGHT

The Seven Deadly Sins of Transforming Commitments

THE PRECEDING CHAPTERS discussed ways to increase your odds of success. You can diagnose your company's susceptibility to active inertia and identify the specific blinders, millstones, routines, shackles, and dogmas that weigh down your organization (as discussed in chapters 2 and 3). You can select an appropriate anchor to pull your organization out of active inertia (chapters 4 and 5). You can determine whether you yourself can do the job or whether someone else should lead the charge, and how to communicate the commitments more persuasively (chapter 6). You can further increase your odds of success by ensuring your transforming commitments are credible, clear, and courageous (chapter 7).

All of these actions increase the likelihood of success. Transforming commitments remain risky business, however. Attempts to break out of active inertia can derail for any number of reasons, including time pressure, lack of resources, or just plain bad luck. But patterns of failure do emerge. Over the past decade, I have studied dozens of transformational efforts directly through research and consulting, as well as students' master's theses, case studies, and histories by other scholars. In studying these cases, I have observed a small number of common mistakes that managers consistently make. I call them the seven deadly sins of transforming commitments because any one of them can kill a transformation. Most are *errors of commission*—actions that managers should *not* have taken but did anyway. Others are *errors of omission*—actions that a manager *should* have taken but failed to. The seven deadly sins are not mutually exclusive. Managers can, and sometimes do, make mistakes simultaneously with unpleasant results.

By and large, the stories in this chapter do not end happily. I include them not as indictments of weak management but as illustrations of ineffectual transformation. Change is risky business. In some cases, I have omitted the names of lesser-known companies to protect their confidentiality. I have included transformation efforts that failed very publicly—Enron, Tyco, Kmart, and AT&T—but I fully acknowledge that the causes of their woes are complex and, in some cases, allegedly criminal. Saving these companies would have been a tall order for even the best of managers. In this chapter, I hope only to codify what we have learned from past failures so that managers can avoid making the same mistakes.

1. Repeat What Worked Last Time

When companies need radical change, directors sometimes hire a manager who has led a successful transformation effort in another company.[1] The benefits of hiring a battle-hardened veteran are obvious. They understand the challenges inherent in breaking a company out of active inertia, and may even have a field-tested handbook for leading the effort.

The danger arises, of course, when a manager attempts to use the same handbook in a different context. Consider the case of Gil Amelio, who replaced Michael Spindler as the CEO of Apple Computer.[2] Amelio, an Apple board member, took the reins after a successful transformation of National Semiconductor. Amelio wrote a book about his experience entitled *Profit from Experience*, in which he detailed his approach for reviving troubled companies. Key components of the approach included involving all employees in all key decisions, encouraging mavericks, avoiding hasty decisions on critical issues, and using layoffs (which Amelio described as "a sign of management failure") only as a last resort.

Amelio followed his playbook inside Apple. He hired former colleagues from National Semiconductor to staff key positions on his management team. He soon learned that what worked so well at National Semiconductor worked poorly at Apple. Involving everyone and encouraging mavericks simply reinforced the highly individualistic culture at Apple. The policy of avoiding hasty decisions apparently contributed to Apple's delay in killing the Newton. The policy of minimal layoffs early on forced Apple to stage a second and larger round of personnel cuts later. Amelio left Apple after seventeen months, when cofounder Steve Jobs returned.

Like his predecessor, Amelio found himself in a tough spot at Apple, caught between a dysfunctional culture and the Wintel juggernaut. His attempts to reenact his victories at National Semiconductor, however, certainly contributed to his difficulties at Apple. Similarly, "Chainsaw" Al Dunlap had led turnarounds at several companies, including Lily-Tulip, Crown-Zellerbach, and Scott Paper, and created significant value for shareholders. Dunlap honed a recipe for leading these turnarounds that included bringing in a SWAT team of experienced managers and consultants, cutting staff deeply, and selling the company quickly.[3] When Dunlap tried to repeat his tried-and-true approach at Sunbeam but could not sell the company quickly according to plan, he resorted to manipulating Sunbeam's accounting figures.

Now consider Kmart.[4] The retailer hired a president from Wal-Mart who cut prices to compete head-to-head with his former employer. What worked for low-cost Wal-Mart, however, hurt high-cost Kmart and contributed to the company's slide into bankruptcy. The problems at Kmart, like those at Apple and Sunbeam, ran deep, and no easy fixes presented themselves. Repeating what worked in a different context looks like an easy fix, but can be a disaster.

Lou Gerstner avoided this mistake. When he joined IBM, Gerstner resisted calls to articulate his grand vision for reviving Big Blue. Instead, he spent time listening to customers, employees, and industry experts to understand what was required in IBM's specific situation. The ultimate commitment of providing integrated customer solutions looked very different from the branding that had worked for Gerstner at RJR-Nabisco. But these were very different companies, and Gerstner recognized that one size did not fit both.

2. Fail to Run the Numbers

Every manager worth her salt recognizes that transformation requires organizational change and often demands strategic repositioning. However, managers often neglect the financial implications of transformation and fail to run the numbers. Focusing on the soft side of transformation while underemphasizing the hard financing can derail otherwise sound transformation efforts.

Consider Enron.[5] In light of Enron's well-publicized bankruptcy, we can easily forget what a remarkable transformation the company achieved. In fifteen years, Enron moved from an interstate gas transmission company to a leading energy trading firm. The transformation positioned the company to seize opportunities in newly deregulated energy markets. Along the way, Ken Lay and Jeff Skilling successfully transformed the company's frames, resources, processes, relationships, and values from those suitable for a regulated utility to a success formula widely admired for its innovation and flexibility. In terms of strategic positioning and organizational change, their transformation of Enron was remarkable.

The company's problems, in my opinion, resulted largely from a failure to clearly think through the financial implications of the transformation. Enron's model consisted of creating markets—in segments such as gas and electricity—where none existed. Because buyers and sellers had imperfect information about one another, Enron could earn a fat commission on the deals they brokered. The very act of creating a market, however, decreased the margins that Enron and other brokers could earn on transactions. Bringing more buyers and sellers together and providing information on previous transactions closed the gap between bids and ask prices on deals, which lowered the margins available to matchmakers. In this situation, Enron faced three basic alternatives. First, it could accept lower margins, but that would conflict with its public claims. Second, it could try to make markets in other commodities, ranging from pulp and paper to pollution-emission allowances. Enron pursued this strategy, and some of these initiatives succeeded despite taking Enron outside its area of expertise in energy.

Third, Enron could bet big on thinner percentage margins to maintain the same level of absolute profits—in effect, to become a hedge fund. Larger bets, however, required larger amounts of capital. Had Enron gone to investors and announced, "We are now a hedge fund," the company would have endangered its high P/E ratio. Enron resorted to off-balance-sheet borrowing to access capital without clearly stating how much money Enron needed to generate its returns. The Enron story, as we all know, is very complicated, and it will be years before we piece together all the elements that contributed to its dramatic fall. Failure to think through the financial implications of the transformation, however, played an important role.

Failing to calculate the costs of transformation and secure the required funding is a common pitfall. Kmart's decision to match Wal-Mart's lower prices was a bold commitment, but also a large investment in forgone profits. Michael Armstrong attempted to

FIGURE 8-1

Run the Numbers of Transformation

What are the financial implications of alternative scenarios?

- What are the projected cash flows if the transformation succeeds? What are the odds of success? What has to go right to succeed? What are the key assumptions driving the model?

- What are the projected cash flows if the transformation fails? What are the odds of failure? What could go wrong to lead to failure?

- What are projected cash flows of maintaining the status quo? How long are they sustainable?

- What are projected cash flows of milking the core business? What investments could be saved? How long are the cash flows sustainable?

- Are there other options we should consider? Leveraged buyout? Sale to strategic buyer?

How much would the transformation cost?

- What are the drivers of the cost? Increases in working capital? R&D? Advertising? Capital spending? Acquisitions? Lost profits in core business?

- Could we sequence the actions to minimize up front costs—for example, small acquisitions before large ones?

How will we finance the transformation?

- Could it be financed with internally generated cash flow? Divestment? Cost-cutting efforts? Reductions in working capital?

- If outside funding is necessary, what is the best source of funds? Bank loans? Issue bonds? Issue equity? What do they bring in addition to money—for example, pressure for change?

- Should we tap capital markets in our home country? Global markets?

- What is happening in the capital markets right now? Is this the right time to raise financing? What are the pros and cons of waiting?

- What is the story we will tell to potential investors and lenders? How will they react? Are investors interested in transformation stories right now?

transform AT&T from a long-distance carrier into an integrated supplier of long-distance, local, and Internet services to end users. His transformation floundered, however, on the $65 billion in debt AT&T took on to acquire cable companies to provide these services. Daewoo's chairman Kim Woo-Choong issued over $10 billion in high-yield bonds when he could no longer secure government funding, leaving his company vulnerable when expected profits failed to materialize. Vivendi's transformation unwound largely because Jean-Marie Messier piled on $17 billion in debt to fund acquisitions of Canal-Plus, the entertainment assets of USA

Networks, and other properties deemed integral to his vision of an integrated media company.

Managers can deliberately avoid a similar fate. Most important, they can recognize that a transformation poses not only organizational and strategic challenges, but also thorny financing issues. Second, they can get help from a seasoned CFO. In every successful transformation in my sample, the manager has worked with a hard-nosed financial expert to debate about required funds, wring free cash from the organization, and identify the appropriate sources of external funding. Transformation requires a pit-bull CFO who is aggressive in asking the hard questions and tenacious in dislodging necessary cash. Lapdogs need not apply. Finally, managers and their financial advisors can ask several questions about the financial side of the transformation. (See figure 8-1.)

3. Don't Sweat the Details

One common mistake that managers make is to select an anchor, hammer it in, and then relax. They fail to plan for the realignment of the existing frames, resources, processes, relationships, and values. The owner of an Argentinean textile company made this mistake. The firm had historically sold high-quality cotton fabric in bulk to dealers, who then resold the cloth to high-end clothing makers in the United States and Western Europe. Faced with low-priced Asian imports, the owner committed to a stretch relationship by bypassing his distributors and forging alliances with the clothing makers. He burned his bridges behind him by severing ties to distributors and entering into direct competition with them. His commitment was clear—sell directly to fashion houses—and credible, and it marked a sharp break with the company's past.

New challenges quickly emerged. The fashion houses required shorter production runs and gave shorter notice when they needed fabric. These new demands taxed the company's production and logistics processes, which were optimized for long runs.

When middle managers raised these issues, the owner dismissed them impatiently, ordering them to sort out these details so that he could manage his relationships with the new customers.

Middle managers quickly concluded that the owner disdained the day-to-day decisions necessary to deliver on his bold promise. They did their best to address the new challenges, but in the end, production costs, inventory levels, and defects grew out of control. The owner had to retreat and return to distributors—tail between his legs.

Another example comes from a midsized U.S. insurance firm. Historically, the firm sold insurance policies, and underwriters earned a commission on new policies written. An outside CEO committed to a new strategic direction and declared the insurer would henceforth provide advisory services. He set aggressive revenue targets for the fledgling advisory services. However, the CEO largely ignored the details of making good on his commitment. A fee-based business must compensate employees based on utilization levels rather than sales commissions. The switch in compensation required new systems to track time spent by client and shifts in the underwriters' take-home pay. The CEO avoided dealing with these nitty-gritty issues of time-tracking software and compensation policy, preferring to spend his time on the big-picture strategic issues of repositioning the company as a risk-management service provider. The transformation initiative failed.

We might dismiss these executives as bad managers, but the truth is more subtle. Selecting the appropriate anchor requires strategic insight and securing it requires boldness. To align the rest of the organization, however, the manager must concentrate on the myriad adjustments that result from the initial actions. What executive committee would ask a manager to combine insight and boldness with disciplined execution? Yet this combination is exactly what the task requires.

How can you avoid this trap? Directors or executives selecting a new CEO, senior managers, or a business unit head should probably look for candidates who have the boldness to break with the past and the discipline to see the changes through. Big-picture insight matters; but most of the effective leaders in my study succeeded by recognizing a good anchor when they saw it, committing to the change, and then executing it relentlessly. With the exception of Lars Kolind at Oticon, none of the successful transformational leaders I have studied came up with the anchor themselves. Asahi's Hirotaro Higuchi initially resisted dry beer, Chuck Pilliod got religion on radials after seeing them roll through Europe, and Marvin Bower recognized the benefit of professionalism based on his training as a lawyer. Their real contributions came from throwing their willpower and detail-oriented execution skills behind the chosen anchor.

Too much big-picture thinking at the expense of detailed execution can hinder the progress of a transformation effort. Recall how Michael Spindler's "fire-hose" approach of spraying out new ideas and directions without following through aggravated Apple's problems. If you consider yourself a bold, creative strategist, then you should consider how you would handle the inevitable deluge of operational problems that follow a bold commitment. A good CFO and COO will help, but you may also consider whether you are the right person to lead the charge.

4. Delegate the Hard Work

Making a bold commitment will surface challenges in making good on the pledge. Solving these challenges, in turn, requires difficult decisions, such as exiting legacy businesses or laying off loyal employees. Faced with such hard calls, some managers try to delegate. I have seen managers attempt this in several ways:

- Owner of a family business hired a professional manager to lead the charge.
- CEO empowered a "transformation committee" of senior executives to develop and implement a plan to change the company.

- Divisional president of a large subsidiary within a public corporation hired a consulting firm specializing in change management to lead the transformation.
- Founder and CEO of a high-technology company asked the COO to lead the transformation in response to shifting technology.
- Managing director of a midsized consulting partnership created a "change committee" to propose and enact a vision for the firm's future.

These efforts have one thing in common. They all failed. One of the hard truths about transforming commitments is that managers cannot outsource the tough calls. Consider the family-owned seafood company based in Maine. The firm bought fresh lobster, crab, and shrimp from commercial fishermen and sold it to national distributors who served grocery stores. A handful of distributors controlled the channels and could beat up their suppliers on price. Fluctuations in supply meant that the seafood company's profits were not only razor-thin, but volatile to boot. When recession hit the Maine economy in 1991, local banks threatened to restrict access to cash just as customer demand for luxuries like crab and lobster was dropping.

The owner hired a consultant, who proposed bypassing the powerful distributors and shipping fresh lobster directly to large regional supermarket chains. The owner liked the plan and hired the consultant as a VP to implement it.

Long-time employees fought the commitment vehemently. Historically, success in the business resulted from personal relationships with distributors, which were lubricated with heavy drinking (and the occasional barroom brawl). Overnight, these relationships were rendered irrelevant. To add insult to injury, employees were asked to follow a set of systematic procedures for purchasing, tracking profits, shipping, and managing inventory. The opponents banded together and approached the owner, who then proceeded to broker a compromise between the new vice president and the old guard. The company ended up pursuing both approaches half-heartedly. The recently hired VP and a few of his allies left the company, which went out of business three years later.

This example illustrates the difficulties of trying to delegate transformation. The owner, CEO, founder, or division manager stands on the sidelines and fails to personally commit to the transformation. Opponents within the organization recognize that they can safely oppose or ignore the commitments. The leader looks like a referee rather than the captain of the team. Outsourcing does preserve plausible deniability—the manager can backpedal from subordinates' commitments, claiming they were nothing more than "trial balloons." The benefit of wriggle room is dwarfed, however, by the associated costs. The employees and managers who stuck their necks out grow cynical and often leave the company. If the manager does get serious about transformation at a later date, he will find it much harder to win converts. These outsourced efforts burn time, resources, and effort that could prove decisive when the leader personally commits to transformation.

5. Half-Tackles

When managers make transforming commitments, they uncover a host of obstacles. Recall, for example, how Lou Gerstner's pledge to provide customer solutions exposed limitations in IBM's organization and gaps in the company's portfolio of products and services. Gerstner, of course, tackled these challenges. Not all managers do. Some make a bold commitment, recognize the problems that emerge, but stop short of taking them on. Anyone who has watched kids playing soccer has seen an analogous pattern. When playing defense, a young child will often see an attacker coming, run full-speed ahead toward the striker, then stop at the last minute and simply stare at the attacker without tackling her. Half-tackles on the soccer field can be pretty entertaining, but they are a disaster in the boardroom or the executive suite.

Managers often make half-tackles when a transforming commitment requires them to sever long-standing relationships with customers, distributors, or suppliers. The saga of a manager of the private banking division of a large German bank illustrates how a transformation can grind to a halt when it collides with established relationships. The new manager committed to transforming his division by wooing high-net-worth clients. Sounds pretty sensible, but there was a hitch. Focusing on the most profitable clients required each private banker to calculate profit per client and prioritize their accounts based on their potential for big fees. The new manager set guidelines on how much time a banker could spend with clients in each category. The private bankers finally balked at the idea of not returning phone calls to clients, some of whom they had served for decades, just because the bank had relegated these clients to a lower category. Faced with resistance, the manager retreated, and the initiative quietly died.

A common form of half-tackle occurs when managers aggressively invest—in new technology, capacity expansion, or acquisitions—to pursue their commitment but are slow to divest assets inconsistent with their future path. The result is that an effort at transformation slips into active inertia. Recall how Firestone's managers delayed closing factories that produced tires no one wanted to buy. The cost of delays in closing these factories, by my estimate, exceeded $300 million, which exceeded the price tag for the Firestone 500 recall. Apple executives postponed killing the Newton, Kmart managers have been slow to close money-losing stores, and Laura Ashley executives dragged their heels in closing the uncompetitive Welsh production facilities.

Delaying exit can bleed a company white. The most obvious cost is financial resources. Delays drain financial resources vital to fulfilling a new commitment. Prolonging an exit also saps management time and attention. Top executives waste endless hours analyzing, discussing the issues, and deploying talented employees to fix the situation, when cutting losses would work better. Finally, long delays erode employees' confidence in management's mettle for making tough calls.

Slow exits are easy to understand. Most companies use a bottom-up process to make investment decisions. Front-line employees propose ideas, middle managers provide impetus, and top executives (and the board) review the projects.[6] This bottom-up process tends to stall when companies really should divest or exit. Few middle managers or front-line employees walk into their bosses' office and volunteer their unit for closure or sale. Managers shy from hurting the employees and communities affected by an exit.

To accelerate exit, the manager leading the charge must often consolidate the investment process and manage it from the top. Recall, for instance, how Oticon's Lars Kolind took budget approval into his own hands. Managers may hasten exit by committing to a stretch relationship with investors. Brian Pitman's commitment to shareholders helped Lloyds TSB pull out of unrelated businesses and international operations while competitors like National Westminster dawdled. Investors may not know what business to get into, but they are pretty good at knowing what business to exit.

6. Ignore Core Values

One deadly mistake occurs when a manager attempts to transform an organization in a manner that runs directly counter to a set of deeply held values. To make this mistake, the manager need not explicitly commit to a new set of values. Managers who commit to a new strategic frame, set of relationships, resources, or processes sometimes take actions that conflict with core values. Trampling on core values inspires a backlash from employees, customers, business partners, and owners. If this backlash gains enough momentum, it can unseat the leader and halt the transformation.

When John Scully attempted to impose financial and operating discipline at Apple, his attempts clashed with Apple's deeply ingrained culture. Technical prima donnas joined Apple to work on the coolest new technology, not to hit quarterly budget numbers.

One outside CEO attempted to reverse Laura Ashley's fortunes by updating the brand to appeal to younger working women. The new line included stark black outfits whose only concession to Laura Ashley's frilly tradition was an inconspicuous flower emblem. The new offerings alienated many faithful customers and franchisees who remained deeply committed to the traditional values embodied in Laura Ashley's genteel country fashion.

The recent demise of Arthur Andersen also illustrates a transformation that ran aground because it ran counter to core values.[7] Arthur Andersen built the firm that bore his name on the bedrock of professional probity. When his fledgling firm was a year old, Andersen told a client that "there isn't enough money in the city of Chicago" to persuade the firm to sign off on a questionable transaction. By 1979, Arthur Andersen had grown to become one of the largest professional services firms in the world, based largely on the partners' reputation for impeccable integrity in audits. Throughout the 1980s, however, the firm earned an increasingly large portion of its profits from consulting work. With the consulting arm breaking off into a separate entity named Accenture in 1998, the remaining auditing partners attempted to transform Arthur Andersen into a diversified professional service firm. The firm adopted a "2X rule" in which audit partners had to bring in twice as much revenue from other services as from the core auditing business. The pressure for nonaudit revenues undermined the founder's values of independence and integrity. Arthur Andersen was implicated in a series of high-profile accounting disputes, including Waste Management Inc., Sunbeam, Boston Market, the Baptist Foundation of Arizona, and, of course, Enron.

Thomas Middelhoff's attempt to remake the German media giant Bertelsmann AG illustrates a transformation that ran aground when it conflicted with the owners' values.[8] Founded in 1835 as a publisher of hymnals, Bertelsmann grew to be the fifth-largest media group in the world, including such properties as Random House, BMG, *Inc.* magazine, and the European broadcaster RTL. The founding family retained control over the private company throughout the twentieth century, and Reinhard Mohn—

a descendant of founder Carl Bertelsmann—presided over the family's interest for decades. Mohn carefully protected the founder's values of social responsibility. As the Bertelsmann Group entered diverse businesses, Mohn also instituted the value of fierce autonomy among the business units.

When Thomas Middelhoff became CEO of Bertelsmann in 1997, he committed to a bold strategy of media convergence, involving magazines, music, books, and the Internet. He invested in online properties, including Bertelsmann online, barnesandnoble.com, CDNow, and Napster. Middelhoff attempted to centralize the independent media fiefdoms with the Bertelsmann confederation to accelerate convergence. He pushed hard for a public offering of the company's stock.

In contrast to Jean-Marie Messier, who followed a similar strategy at Vivendi, Middelhoff did *not* run into financial difficulties. Rather, the owners perceived his aggressive push to centralize power and recast Bertelsmann as a typical public media company as a threat to its core values. The owners removed Middelhoff.

7. Keep Past Sell-By Date

People often think of commitments as lasting forever. Some personal commitments, such as marriage vows or religious orders, are indeed meant to last a lifetime. Enduring vows, however, are a dangerous analogy in business. We have seen how the defining commitments that enabled early success can harden over time and later hinder organizations from responding effectively when the environment shifts. One surprising finding from my research is that transforming commitments, like defining commitments, have a shelf life. The same ruthless logic applies to the bold commitments that managers make to hoist their organizations from active inertia.

Consider Eckhard Pfeiffer's transformation of Compaq Computer in the early 1990s.[9] In the wake of Compaq's recent travails, you might not think of Compaq as a success. But turn back the clock and recall the company that Pfeiffer inherited in October 1991. In that year, the company had missed analysts' earnings targets in two consecutive quarters, announced its first-ever quarterly loss, and laid off fourteen hundred employees. Compaq had lost market share for two straight years and watched its market share drop by half in a single year.

Between 1991 and 1998, CEO Pfeiffer completely transformed Compaq and drove revenues from slightly over $3 billion in 1991 to $31 billion seven years later. These dramatic increases in revenues and improved cash flows drove the company's market capitalization from $2 billion at the end of 1991 to nearly $71 billion at the end of 1998, handily outperforming the NASDAQ index during that period and dwarfing the few billion dollars created by founder Rod Canion.[10] Within three years of Pfeiffer's taking charge, Compaq surpassed leader IBM in PC market share.

Pfeiffer committed to a new strategic direction when he reframed the company's target market from *Fortune* 100 buyers to include all segments of the market, including the small businesses and consumers that Compaq had historically disdained. Pfeiffer secured his commitment by translating it into concrete goals, publicly pledging to meet these goals, and by backing up his promises with bold actions that lent credibility to his commitment. Three months after replacing Canion, for example, Pfeiffer declared that Compaq would meet any competitor on price, and several months later, pledged that Compaq would be the leading supplier of PCs and servers worldwide by 1996. In June 1992, Compaq announced a 32 percent across-the-board price cut and introduced two new lines of inexpensive computers.

Pfeiffer focused ruthlessly on the details necessary to deliver on his promises. He shifted the company's sights on local rival Dell to rally the troops to beat the low-cost clones; he instituted volume-based metrics to measure success; and he forged new relationships with consumer and small-business resellers. Pfeiffer successfully transformed Compaq from a niche producer of pricey PCs for *Fortune* 100 companies to the largest volume producer in the industry. His remarkable transformation landed Pfeiffer on the cover of *Forbes* magazine when Compaq was named the company of the year for 1997. As we saw in chapter 3, such billing can be a bad sign, and the board fired Pfeiffer less than two years later.

The causes of Compaq's problems in the late 1990s are, of course, complicated, but Pfeiffer's transforming commitments contributed to the company's woes. The clear commitment to volume (and the associated volume-based metrics) hardened into a quota mentality where employees equated success with boxes shipped. The obsessive focus on Dell and other clone-makers blinded Compaq managers to the resurgent IBM's strategy of providing integrated customer solutions. Relationships with distributors had become shackles that prevented the company from emulating Dell's direct model. Compaq ended up caught in active inertia; it could neither sell machines cheaply enough to beat Dell nor emulate IBM and provide integrated customer solutions.

The danger of sticking with a transforming commitment beyond its sell-by date is particularly high in fast-moving industries. Managers who are aware of this risk, however, will less likely let their own transforming commitments harden into future sources of active inertia.

––––––––––

Managers who recognize the pitfalls described in this chapter are more likely to avoid them. Chapter 9 helps managers think through the personal side of their professional commitments.

NINE

The Private Side of Public Commitments

Before making transforming commitments, you need good answers to several questions: Is your company suffering from active inertia? Are transforming commitments right for your company? *Which* anchor suits your specific situation? Are *you* the right person for the job? Can you make your commitments stick? Can you avoid common mistakes?

As we have seen, managers *can* successfully transform established organizations. Making bold commitments, however, requires managers to stick their necks out. Making good on these promises demands the tenacity and willpower to overcome the onerous weight of the past. Transforming the status quo demands a personal commitment that feels very different from business as usual. Finally, most managers have alternatives—they can quit or just sit there and hope for the best.

So why commit rather than sit or quit? This question takes us from the impersonal terrain of finance, strategy, and organization and into the personal, which many people prefer to avoid. The boldness and the tenacity to transform an organization require willpower and stamina above and beyond the call of duty—to simply maintain the status quo. Why managers personally commit to transformation could very well be the crux of the story.

Managers cite several reasons for the decision to tackle this level of challenge, and I have listed the most common ones here. There is no "right" answer. There are, however, certain benefits and risks associated with each motivation. Understanding these different rationales may illuminate your own motives.

- *I Didn't Know It Would Be So Hard.* Some managers commit to a company transformation out of ignorance. At the outset, they simply have no idea how hard transforming their company's success formula will be. Ignorance is not bliss for very long in these situations. Managers who do not grasp the enormity of the challenge often give up once the going gets rough. On balance, this answer is probably the most dangerous one that you can give.

- *Our Backs Were Against the Wall.* Managers and boards often make transforming commitments during a crisis. Asahi had suffered a greenmail threat and layoffs just prior to Hirotaro Higuchi's big bet on dry beer. Nokia was on the brink of bankruptcy when Jorma Ollila committed to telecommunications. In a crisis, everyone recognizes that the formula must change. By the time the situation has reached a crisis, however, the company may be left with few good alternatives and depleted resources.

- *It Was a Chance for Glory.* Transformation offers the chance for kudos if successful. Some managers rise to the challenge to make a name for themselves. Lars Kolind's transformation of Oticon, for example, allowed him to succeed on a grand scale. The desire for recognition can lead a manager to commit publicly and, therefore, increase credibility and effectiveness. Recall how Kolind invited the press to document Oticon's move. Desiring recognition without clearly understanding the company's predicament can be dangerous. Outsiders are particularly susceptible to this risk.

- *I Knew the Answer.* Some managers face a crisis, others go for the glory, but some make transforming commitments from a deep conviction that they know the best approach. Marvin Bower, for example, harbored a deep conviction that professionalism was the key to McKinsey's future. Brian Pitman firmly believed that a commitment to shareholders would pull Lloyds TSB from its stagnation. Being certain is great, as long as you are also right. A danger arises, however, when a manager has not worked through the complexity of a company's unique situation but still has "The Answer." Recall how Gil Amelio entered Apple with a clear blueprint for saving Apple based on his experience at National Semiconductor. Certainty can lead managers to ignore signs that the plan is fizzling.

- *It Was Something Worth Fighting For.* Some managers commit to transforming an organization because they value the company's legacy. Steve Jobs certainly didn't return to Apple because he needed the money. Lou Gerstner and many others believed IBM was worth saving because it represented a national treasure.

If you want to preserve a worthwhile legacy, then ask yourself, "What specifically is worth preserving?" You can then eliminate any action that forces you to abandon the valuable elements. Conversely, these things can guide your commitments. Lego CEO Kjell Kristiansen, for example, committed Lego to diversifying into businesses outside its core, as long as the new products took kids seriously, stimulated creativity, and retained the Lego look and feel. The results of Lego's transformation are not in yet, but this approach has the advantage of building on the company's legacy. The risk is that managers will keep the bathwater as well as the baby.

The George Bailey Test

A simple exercise can help you think through the question, "Why should I commit to a major transformation? The test takes its name from the hero of the classic holiday film *It's a Wonderful Life*. Begin by taking out a piece of blank white paper and folding it in three columns.

1. In the first column, list all the benefits that would result if you personally committed and your transformation succeeded. You are reflecting back on all the benefits that resulted. Do not write an essay—bullet points are fine. The goal is neither completeness nor precision. Just list the main benefits here. The following questions may help you to get started on your list:

   - How is the company doing? Relative to competitors? Relative to where it was when you started?

   - How much economic value has been created?

   - How many new jobs were created? Existing jobs preserved?

   - What benefits did members of your management team enjoy? Career-wise? Development? Reputation? Financial?

   - How have you personally benefited in terms of your career? Your reputation? Excitement? Your professional development? Your personal net worth?

2. In the second column, imagine that you made your commitment and it clearly failed. As you did above for the benefits, now do so for the associated costs. That is, just list the main costs:

   - What happened to the company under this scenario? Is it worse off than it would have been had you not attempted the transformation?

- How much value has been destroyed relative to the former status quo?

- How many jobs were lost relative to persisting in the status quo?

- What have been the costs to your team? In terms of career? Professional development? Personal reputation? Net worth?

- What have been the costs to you along the same dimensions?

3. In the third column, imagine that you made no commitment. You are reflecting back on the consequences of your failure to do so. This column gives the exercise its name. In a moment of crisis and despair, George Bailey—the lead character in *It's a Wonderful Life*—wishes that he had never been born. An angel grants his wish and gives him the chance to see how the world fared without him. Some questions to consider:

- What would you do instead of making a transforming commitment? Tweak the existing success formula? Lie low and let someone else worry about the company's challenges? Leave?

- If you choose not to commit, then who will? How does your decision influence the timing of the transformation? Will business pick up later? Can your company afford the delay?

- What are the personal costs to you? Would you wonder if you could have done it? Should have done it? Do you have any regrets?

Managers who walk through this exercise often surprise themselves by concluding that if they choose not to commit to transformation, they cannot say who will instead. Of course, this is not to say that every manager should commit to transforming every organization. Incremental changes to the existing success formula will sometimes suffice. Other times, a leader will conclude that no conceivable actions could possibly save the company and the most responsible course of action is a liquidation or sale. This exercise does highlight, however, that when a company *is* suffering from active inertia, and a manager *does* know what to do and *can* execute, she is often the only person who could.

We can all visualize the costs of failed commitments—tarnished reputation, bad ink in the press, limited career options. But what about the costs of *not* committing? Managers cite costs like *never knowing* whether they could have pulled it off, *regretting their ambivalence* while their company slid into trouble, and *feeling guilty* about not adequately defending the values that attracted them to the organization in the first place.

Why Wait?

Like life in general, the practice of management can be overwhelmingly complex. When the complexity of the challenge paralyzes you, pause to simplify. Many of the major themes in this book fall into three basic questions:

What is the right thing to do? Most managers can answer this question pretty quickly. Of course, there are exceptions— the outsider in a new job and new company, or the entrepreneur in a chaotic industry. In their heart of hearts, however, most managers *know* what to do. Clarity might emerge only after a few days' vacation or the second glass of cabernet sauvignon, but it is there.

What hinders you? If you accept the proposition that you already know the right thing to do in your own company, the interesting question becomes why you haven't done it already. Sometimes the hindrances are external and truly beyond your control. In my conversations with managers, however, I am struck by how often they say the biggest obstacles are internal.

Why wait? If you know what to do and believe that you yourself should do it, then what stops you? Are you waiting for a minor crisis to create your opportunity to act, or are you honing your plan as an inside-outsider? One observation: Whenever I interview a manager who made transforming commitments—successful or not—I always close with the same question, "What would you have done differently?" Almost all reply the same: *I would have started earlier and moved faster than I did.*

So why wait?

INTRODUCTION

1. Donald T. Campbell is generally credited with introducing an explicit evolutionary model into the organizational theory field in his seminal piece, "Variation and Selective Retention in Socio-Cultural Evolution," *General Systems* 14 (1969): 69–85. Howard Aldrich introduced the notion of "imprinting," whereby organizations are stamped at their formation in an organizational mode that resists subsequent change. See Howard E. Aldrich, *Organizations and Environments* (Englewood Cliffs, NJ: Prentice Hall, 1979). Michael Hannan and John Freeman subsequently elaborated the argument of structural inertia and argued that change takes place at the level of the population of organizations rather than within organizations. See Michael Hannan and John Freeman, "The Population Ecology of Organizations," *American Journal of Sociology* 82, no. 5 (1977): 929–964, and "Structural Inertia and Organizational Change," *American Sociological Review* 49, no. 2 (1984): 149–164. A parallel stream of evolutionary thinking emerged in economics concurrently with the research in sociology. The earliest antecedents stretch back to Schumpeter's memorable analysis of capitalism as "creative destruction"; see Joseph A. Schumpeter, *Capitalism, Socialism, and Democracy* (New York: Harper, 1975/1942), 82–85. Armen A. Alchian introduced evolutionary models into neoclassical economics in "Uncertainty, Evolution, and Economic Theory," *Journal of Political Economy* 58 (1950): 211–221. Richard R. Nelson and Sidney G. Winter elaborated an evolutionary model of economic change in *An Evolutionary Theory of Economic Change* (Cambridge, MA: Belknap Press, 1982).

2. See Clayton M. Christensen, *The Innovator's Dilemma: When New Technologies Cause Great Firms to Fail* (Boston: Harvard Business School Press, 1997).

3. See Richard N. Foster and Sarah Kaplan, *Creative Destruction: Why Companies That Are Built to Last Underperform the Market—and How to Successfully Transform Them* (New York: Currency, 2001).

4. See Gary Hamel, *Leading the Revolution* (Boston: Harvard Business School Press, 2000), and Thomas J. Peters, *Thriving on Chaos: Handbook for a Management Revolution* (New York: Knopf, 1987).

5. In some cases, the pairing of direct competitors made it difficult to secure the same level of access to both companies. In these cases, I focused my interviews on the successful companies and relied primarily on public sources for the less successful companies. For the Samsung and Daewoo pairing, I drew on findings from an ongoing study of Korean *chaebol* with Professor Choelsoon Park of Seoul National University. I also served as a paid advisor to Nokia, Ericsson, and Compaq. In some cases, I wrote case studies or articles on the company. For the companies for which I did not publish a case study or article, I have relied exclusively on publicly available information to illustrate points in this book. My understanding of the situation has, of course, been informed by my interviews and time spent with managers in the companies.

6. Many scholars have analyzed the relationship between theory and knowledge, but my own thinking has been most influenced by the philosopher Karl Popper. For an accessible summary that is faithful to Popper's writing, see Bryan Magee, *Philosophy and the Real World: An Introduction to Karl Popper* (LaSalle, IL: Open Court, 1973).

CHAPTER ONE

1. Some psychologists use the construct "organizational commitment" to describe an employee's state of attachment to an organization and have explored the antecedents and consequences of organizational commitment in great detail. For a recent review, see John P. Meyer and Natalie J. Allen, "A Three Component Conceptualization of Organizational Commitment," *Human Resource Management Review* 1 (1991): 64–98. A separate stream of literature has developed the construct of "goal commitment" in reference to a person's attachment to a goal. For a recent review, see Edwin A. Locke, Gary P. Latham, and Miriam Erez, "The Determinants of Goal Commitment," *Academy of Management Review* 13, no. 1 (1998): 23–39.

2. Pankaj Ghemawat initially defined commitment as the "tendency of strategies to persist over time." See Pankaj Ghemawat, *Commitment: The*

Dynamic of Strategy (New York: Free Press, 1991), 14. My construct of commitments maps more closely to Ghemawat's recent definition of commitments as an action—that is, "a few lumpy decisions involving large changes in resource endowments . . . that have significant, lasting effects on firms' future and menus of opportunities or choices," in Pankaj Ghemawat, *Strategy and the Business Landscape* (Upper Saddle River, NJ: Prentice Hall, 2001), 121. The construct of managerial commitments is broader than the notion of a few big bets, however. It includes incremental decisions that cumulatively bind an organization to a course of action. Managerial commitments, as I use the term, also includes actions such as public statements, personnel decisions, and forging relationships with resource providers that are broader than the financial investments and disinvestments on which Ghemawat's analysis focuses.

3. Much of the psychological literature naturally focuses on *individual* commitment, but economists have also explored this level. Jon Elster, for example, frequently frames his discussion in terms of individuals who shape their future behavior to overcome weakness of will. See Jon Elster, "Introduction," in Jon Elster (ed.), *The Multiple Self* (Cambridge, UK: Cambridge University Press, 1985), 1–34. See also Elster's *Ulysses and the Sirens.*

4. For an accessible, concise discussion of commitment in industrial organizational theory, see Garth Saloner, Andrea Shepard, and Joel Podolny, *Strategic Management* (New York: John Wiley, 2001), 416–421. For a more comprehensive, technical overview, see Jean Tirole, *The Theory of Industrial Organization* (Cambridge, MA: MIT Press, 1988).

5. The majority of the research in the escalation of commitment literature has focused on the individual and is based on laboratory experiments. For a recent review of this literature, see Joel Brockner, "The Escalation of Commitment to a Failing Course of Action: Toward Theoretical Progress," *Academy of Management Review* 17, no. 1 (1992): 39–61. Recently, scholars in this tradition have broadened their focus to study escalation at the organizational level. See Jerry Ross and Barry M. Staw, "Organizational Escalation and Exit: Lessons from the Shoreham Nuclear Power Plant," *Academy of Management Journal* 36, no. 4 (1993): 701–732, and Barry M. Staw and Jerry Ross, "Behavior in Escalation Situations: Antecedents, Prototypes, and Solutions," in Barry M. Staw and Lawrence L. Cummings (eds.), *Research in Organizational Behavior* (Greenwich, CT: JAI Press, 1987), Volume 9, 39–78.

6. More precisely, a "managerial commitment" is an action taken by an agent in a time period that increases the probability that the agent's organization will behave in a specified way in subsequent time periods by increas-

ing the future costs of deviating from the specified behavior, up to the limit of excluding altogether the possibility of alternative courses of action. This definition, and particularly the notion of intertemporal binding, is based on the construct of "pre-commitment" used in game theory and defined in Jon Elster, *Ulysses and the Sirens: Studies in Rationality and Irrationality* (Cambridge, UK: Cambridge University Press, 1979), 36–111, especially 39. The term *agent* here is not used in the narrow sense of someone employed by owners of a firm to act on their behalf. See Michael C. Jensen and William H. Meckling, "Theory of the Firm: Managerial Behavior, Agency Costs, and Ownership Structure," *Journal of Financial Economics* 3 (1976): 305–360. Rather, I use the term to describe any person who has the ability to act in a manner that binds the organization.

7. For one attempt at a comprehensive taxonomy, see Elster, *Ulysses and the Sirens,* 103–111.

8. See Ghemawat, *Commitment,* 19–21, and Avinash K. Dixit and Barry J. Nalebuff, *Thinking Strategically: The Competitive Edge in Business, Politics and Everyday Life* (New York: W. W. Norton, 1991), 152–155.

9. Economists have analyzed the role of a firm's reputation in making credible commitments. For an influential early analysis, see Thomas C. Schelling, *The Strategy of Conflict* (Cambridge, MA: Harvard University Press, 1960), 21–52; for an accessible overview, see David M. Kreps, *Game Theory and Economic Modeling* (Oxford, UK: Clarendon Press, 1990), 65–77.

10. Leon Festinger's theory of cognitive dissonance argues that individuals will avoid reversing publicly stated commitments because they are unwilling to admit—to themselves as well as others—that they were wrong in the first place. See Leon Festinger, *A Theory of Cognitive Dissonance* (Evanston, IL: Row, Peterson, 1957). See also Gerald R. Salancik, "Commitment and the Control of Organizational Behavior and Belief," in Barry M. Staw and Gerald R. Salancik (eds.), *New Directions in Organizational Behavior* (Chicago: St. Clair, 1977), 1–54.

11. The distinction between promising to do something and asserting the veracity of a statement builds on a branch of philosophy known as "speech act" theory. Agents, according to this theory, use speech acts to induce listeners to rely on them. Public promises or "commissives" commit a speaker to a future course of action. "Assertives" commit the speaker to the veracity of a statement. By asserting that a statement is true, a speaker induces listeners to rely on her to act in the future as if the statement were indeed true. This can have the indirect effect of locking the speaker into acting in a manner consistent with the ongoing veracity of that statement. For an introduction to speech act theory, see John R. Searle, *Speech Acts* (Cam-

bridge, UK: Cambridge University Press, 1969). For a concise overview of the categories of speech acts, see John R. Searle, *Expression and Meaning: Studies in the Theory of Speech Acts* (Cambridge, UK: Cambridge University Press, 1979), 1–29.

12. The most comprehensive exposition of the resource dependence view is found in Jeffrey Pfeffer and Gerald R. Salancik, *The External Control of Organizations* (New York: Harper & Row, 1978). For a review and exploration of the linkages between resource dependence and institutional theory, see Christine Oliver, "Strategic Responses to Institutional Processes," *Academy of Management Review* 16, no. 1 (1991): 145–179.

13. Clayton Christensen's research in the disk drive industry demonstrates that firms are unlikely to invest in new technologies that are not aligned with the technical trajectory of their current customers. For an accessible overview of his findings, see Clayton M. Christensen, *The Innovator's Dilemma: When New Technologies Cause Great Firms to Fail* (Boston: Harvard Business School Press, 1997). My own research on incumbent tire makers' response to radial technology demonstrates that most tire manufacturers invested heavily to build radial tire capacity to serve the needs of their largest customers. In the tire industry example, it appears that the firms actually *overinvested* to serve the large automobile manufacturers and, in fact, spent heavily on radial tire production capacity despite low projected returns on their investment. See Donald N. Sull, Richard S. Tedlow, and Richard S. Rosenbloom, "Managerial Commitments and Technological Change in the U.S. Tire Industry," *Industrial and Corporate Change* 6, no. 2 (1997): 461–501.

14. See Joseph Farrell and Garth Saloner, "Coordination Through Committees and Markets," *RAND Journal of Economics* 19 (1988): 235–252.

15. Ram Charan and Jerry Useem, "Why Companies Fail," *Fortune*, 27 May 2002, 60.

16. For a discussion of reputation as an enforcement mechanism for incomplete contracts, see Joseph Farrell and Carl Shapiro, "Optimal Contracts with Lock-in," *American Economic Review* 79 (1989): 51–68. For an accessible summary, see Paul R. Milgrom and John Roberts, *Economics, Organizations, and Management* (Englewood Cliffs, NJ: Prentice Hall, 1992), 129–140. Not all contacts are credible as mechanisms to bind an organization, a topic I explore in chapter 7.

17. For a general discussion of how managers use metrics and control systems to steer their organizations, see Robert S. Kaplan and David P. Norton, *The Balanced Scorecard: Translating Strategy into Action* (Boston: Harvard Business School Press, 1996). For a specific discussion of how control

systems can support change, see Robert Simons, *Levers of Control: Systems to Drive Strategic Renewal* (Boston: Harvard Business School Press, 1995). For a more theoretical discussion of manipulation of information as a mechanism for commitment outside the organizational context, see Elster, *Ulysses and the Sirens,* 108 ff.

18. For a review of recent research on incentives as a mechanism to influence behavior, see Milgrom and Roberts, *Economics, Organizations, and Management,* 167–239.

19. Ghemawat, *Commitment,* 81–107.

20. Strategic commitments as a mechanism to beat competitors in zero-sum games is one of the central theoretical pillars of modern industrial organization economics. Economists often employ game theory to model interactions between competitors and to explore how a commitment by one firm will influence the behavior of its current or potential rivals. For an excellent early overview of how historical commitments shape subsequent strategic interaction, see David M. Kreps and A. Michael Spence, "Modeling the Role of History in Industrial Organization and Competition," in George R. Feiwel (ed.), *Contemporary Issues in Modern Microeconomics* (London: Macmillan, 1984). Baumol et al. argue that in markets characterized by ease of entry and exit, firms will be unable to earn profits exceeding their cost of capital because their commitments are incapable of deterring entry. See William J. Baumol, John C. Panzar, and Robert D. Willig, *Contestable Markets and the Theory of Industry Structure* (New York: Harcourt Brace Jovanovich, 1982). The commitment-based school of industrial economics is not without its critics. See Sam Peltzman, "The Handbook of Industrial Organization: A Review Article," *Journal of Political Economy* 99, no. 1 (1991): 201–217. Peltzman's critique focuses on the needless formality of many industrial economics models and the sensitivity of their predictions to initial assumptions. Although these criticisms are justified, in my opinion, they do not undermine the underlying insight that commitments can influence rivals' behavior and thereby have an impact on competitive performance.

21. Not all interactions between firms are zero-sum games, of course, and one of the most important benefits of credible commitments is their ability to induce collaboration in cooperative games—that is, games where both parties are better off if they work together. For an accessible overview of actions managers can take to induce collaboration, see Barry J. Nalebuff and Adam M. Brandenburger, *Co-opetition* (New York: Currency Doubleday, 1996). These commitments can be particularly powerful in markets characterized by "network effects," in which the value of a product or service to one consumer depends in part on the number of other users—for example,

telephones, fax machines, and business exchanges. In such situations, firms often make commitments to induce potential partners to create complementary goods or services that stimulate demand for the firm's own product. For an influential theoretical treatment, see Michael L. Katz and Carl Shapiro, "Network Externalities, Competition and Compatibility," *American Economic Review* 75 (1985): 424–440.

22. The importance of early commitments to gain market share is particularly critical in so-called winner-take-all battles between two incompatible standards—VHS versus beta, color versus black-and-white television—in which one of the standards is likely to win the vast majority of the market. For a technical discussion, see Michael L. Katz and Carl Shapiro, "Systems Competition and Network Effects," *Journal of Economic Perspectives* 8, no. 2 (1994): 93–115. For an accessible overview, see Carl Shapiro and Hal R. Varian, *Information Rules: A Strategic Guide to the Network Economy* (Boston: Harvard Business School Press, 1999). For an empirical analysis, see Thomas R. Eisenmann, "Racing: Performance Consequences for Internet Companies," working paper, Harvard Business School, Boston, 2002.

23. James C. Collins and Jerry I. Porras, *Built to Last* (New York: HarperBusiness, 1996); Locke et al., "The Determinants of Goal Commitment"; and Salancik, "Commitment and the Control of Organizational Behavior and Belief."

24. Robert K. Merton introduced the term "self-fulfilling prophecy" into organizational studies in *Social Theory and Social Structure* (1948; reprint, New York: Free Press, 1968), 475–490. Merton argued, "if men define situations as real, they are real in their consequences," but framed the self-fulfilling prophecy as a negative dynamic and did not explore its potential benefits. Nor did he explore the role commitments might play in triggering and sustaining self-fulfilling prophecies. Subsequent research on self-fulfilling prophecies has focused more narrowly on how supervisors increase the performance of subordinates by holding high performance expectations. See Dov Eden, "Self-fulfilling Prophecy as a Management Tool: Harnessing Pygmalion," *Academy of Management Review* 9, no. 1 (1984): 64–74.

25. Dorothy Leonard-Barton, "Core Capabilities and Core Rigidities: A Paradox in Managing New Product Development," *Strategic Management Journal* 13 (1992): 111–125.

26. For an early discussion of how managers' commitments can hinder them from responding to crises, see Richard G. Hamermesh, "Responding to Divisional Profit Crises," *Harvard Business Review,* March–April 1977, 24–30. See also Brockner, "The Escalation of Commitment to a Failing Course of Action."

27. Philip Selznick first argued that managers' early commitments can impair the organization's ability to survive under new environmental conditions. See Philip Selznick, *Leadership in Administration* (Berkeley: University of California Press, 1984), 18.

28. Larry E. Greiner published the seminal piece on organizational life cycles. See Larry E. Greiner, "Evolution and Revolution as Organizations Grow," *Harvard Business Review,* July–August 1972, 37–76. Subsequent scholars explored the life cycle model in greater detail. See John R. Kimberly and Robert H. Miles, *The Organizational Life Cycle* (San Francisco: Jossey-Bass, 1980). For a recent review of life cycle theories, see Andrew H. Van de Ven and Marshall Scott Poole, "Explaining Development and Change in Organizations," *Academy of Management Review* 20, no. 3 (1995): 510–540. Empirical analysis supported the hypothesis that firms could be described as passing sequentially through a series of predictable stages. See Danny Miller and Peter H. Friesen, "Momentum and Revolution in Organizational Adaptation," *Academy of Management Journal* 23 (1980): 591–614, and Robert Drazin and Robert K. Kazanjian, "A Reanalysis of Miller and Friesen's Lifecycle Data," *Strategic Management Journal* 11 (1990): 319–325. Although this stream of research describes stages in the life cycle and supports the hypothesis that firms pass through them, it provides few insights on the underlying microprocesses that might explain life cycles.

29. Philip Selznick uses the term "character-defining commitment" to describe decisions that affect a company's capacity to control its future behavior. See Selznick, *Leadership in Administration,* 35 and 55. Although Selznick's treatment is very brief, he seems to imply that these commitments can occur at any stage in an organization's existence (p. 35) and that they refer primarily to decisions on values (p. 55). Defining commitments, as I use the term, is a narrower construct inasmuch as it is limited to those actions that contribute to the initial formation of the structure versus later commitments. It is broader, however, in that commitments need not be limited to a set of values.

30. Reinforcing commitments bear some resemblance to Howard Becker's construct of "side bets." See Howard S. Becker, "Notes on the Concept of Commitment," *American Journal of Sociology* 66 (1960): 32–40. Becker argues that an individual makes a side bet when he "has staked something of value to him, originally unrelated to his present line of action, on being consistent in his present behavior" (p. 35). Becker uses the term "commitment by default" (p. 38) to explain how individuals often make a series of small unconscious side bets that reinforce their current line of activity. Reinforcing commitments is a broader notion, however, because it also

encompasses large, bet-the-company decisions that reinforce the existing organization's strategic frames, resources, processes, relationships, and values. The distinction between defining and reinforcing commitments does not hinge on their magnitude or whether they were made consciously. Rather, the distinction rests on whether they initially define or subsequently reinforce an organization's frames, resources, processes, relationships, and values.

31. The data in this section draws on a series of articles I published analyzing the history of the U.S. tire industry. To avoid repeated self-citation, I will not footnote my sources for the tire industry data but describe these articles here. For a history of the tire industrial clusters centered in Akron, Ohio, from its inception in the 1880s through the 1980s, see Donald N. Sull, "From Community of Innovation to Community of Inertia: The Rise and Fall of the Akron Tire Cluster," working paper 01-025, Harvard Business School, Boston, 2001. For an in-depth analysis of a single company's response to radial tire technology, see Donald N. Sull, "The Dynamics of Standing Still: Firestone Tire & Rubber and the Radial Revolution," *Business History Review* 73, no. 3 (1999): 430–464. For a comparative case study of how the five largest incumbent tire producers responded to radial tires, see Donald N. Sull, Richard S. Tedlow, and Richard S. Rosenbloom, "Managerial Commitments and Technological Change in the U.S. Tire Industry," *Industrial and Corporate Change* 6, no. 2 (1997): 461–501.

32. Howard Stevenson argues that entrepreneurial management is characterized by the tendency to commit resources in sequentially increasing stages rather than large up-front investments. See Howard H. Stevenson, "A Perspective on Entrepreneurship," in William A. Sahlman et al. (eds.), *The Entrepreneurial Venture* (Boston: Harvard Business School Press, 1999), 7–22. Stevenson's argument focuses on commitments that I would classify as investments of capital, but the staging argument applies to other types of commitments as well. An entrepreneur might engage a potential employee as a consultant, for example, before hiring her permanently. While entrepreneurs may prefer to stage their commitments, they cannot avoid making them altogether. In order to attract necessary resources in the formative years of a company, entrepreneurs may be forced to publicly commit to a single strategy or enter into an undiversified resource dependency relationship with customers or investors.

33. There is a growing body of literature on how shared cognitive models influence the behavior of managers and employees. For the most part, this literature has focused on the shared models within established companies. For the seminal piece, see Joseph F. Porac, Howard Thomas, and Charles Baden-Fuller, "Competitive Groups as Cognitive Communities: The

Case of Scottish Knitwear Manufacturers," *The Journal of Management Studies* 26, no. 4 (1989): 397–416. We know much less about how entrepreneurs initially define strategic frames in the formative years of a business.

34. The broad definition of resources to include tangible and intangible assets draws on the resource-based view of the firm. See Birger Wernerfelt, "A Resource Based View of the Firm," *Strategic Management Journal* 5, no. 2 (1984): 171–180. There is some ambiguity about the definition of "resource," specifically, what does and does not fall within the definition. Some authors include processes and relationships as resources, for example, while others would exclude these. For the sake of conceptual clarity, I adopt a tight specification of resources as factors that can be bought and sold, albeit imperfectly, on factor markets. This narrower definition excludes a firm's shared cognitive frames, processes, relationships with external resource providers, and normative values. This tighter definition is consistent with the "dynamic capability view" of the firm that emphasizes how resources are deployed, rather than expertise in picking resources, as a source of quasi-rents. See David J. Teece, Gary P. Pisano, and Amy Shuen, "Dynamic Capabilities and Strategic Management," *Strategic Management Journal* 18, no. 7 (1997): 509–533. Research in the dynamic capability stream clearly distinguishes between resources that can be bought and sold and a firm's capabilities to deploy these resources (generally in combination) using an organizational process. See Raphael Amit and Paul J. H. Schoemaker, "Strategic Assets and Organizational Rent," *Strategic Management Journal* 14, no. 1 (1993), 33–46.

35. Ghemawat, *Commitment*, 18.

36. Ghemawat's definition of sticky resources as durable, specialized, and difficult to trade differs somewhat from the characteristics of a resource according to the resource-based view of the firm—that is, rare, valuable, difficult to substitute, and difficult to imitate by other firms. See Jay B. Barney, "Firm Resources and Sustained Competitive Advantage," *Journal of Management* 17, no. 1 (1991): 99–120. The difference results, in my opinion, because these authors are addressing related but slightly different questions. Ghemawat asks, "What are the characteristics of resources that lock a firm into a persistent strategy?" Authors in the resource-based view, in contrast, address the question of what accounts for sustainable differences in firms' performance. The resource-based-view authors, as a result, include the criterion "valuable" to explain how these resources contribute to firm performance and scarcity and "inimitability" to explain why competitors do not quickly acquire the same resources. For a recent synthesis of the commitment and resource-based views, see Pankaj Ghemawat, "Competition and

Business Strategy in Historical Perspective," *Business History Review* 76 (Spring 2002): 37–74. I use Ghemawat's definition because my interest, like his, is primarily in what factors bind an organization to a behavior over time.

37. The study of processes within organizations extends at least as far back as Frederick Taylor and has been recently elaborated by influential scholars such as Richard R. Nelson and Sidney G. Winter, *An Evolutionary Theory of Economic Change* (Cambridge, MA: Belknap, 1982). Scholars have analyzed a series of specific processes; for literature on decision processes, see Chester I. Barnard, *The Functions of the Executive* (Cambridge, MA: Harvard University Press, 1938) and Herbert A. Simon, *Administrative Behavior* (New York: Macmillan, 1945); for capital budgeting, see Joseph L. Bower, *Managing the Resource Allocation Process* (Boston: Harvard Business School Press, 1974); for new venture creation, see Robert A. Burgelman, "A Process Model of Internal Corporate Venturing in the Diversified Major Firm," *Administrative Science Quarterly* 28, no. 2 (1983): 223–244; and for new product development, see Steven C. Wheelwright and Kim B. Clark, *Revolutionizing Product Development* (New York: Free Press, 1992). For a comprehensive review of process research, see David A. Garvin, "The Processes of Organization and Management," *Sloan Management Review* 39, no. 4 (Summer 1998): 33–50.

38. For a comprehensive discussion of the competitive benefits of committing to a set of processes, see Nelson and Winter, *An Evolutionary Theory of Economic Change*, 96–136.

39. Michael Hannan and John H. Freeman, "Structural Inertia and Organizational Change," *American Sociological Review* 49, no. 2 (1984): 149–164.

40. Joel M. Podolny, "A Status-Based Model of Market Competition," *American Journal of Sociology* 98, no. 4 (1993): 829–872.

41. See Jeffrey H. Dyer and Harbir Singh, "The Relational View: Cooperative Strategy and Sources of Interorganizational Competitive Advantage," *Academy of Management Review* 23 (1988): 660–679.

42. For an excellent review of the literature on hierarchical versus market relationships, see Oliver E. Williamson, *The Economic Institutions of Capitalism: Firms, Markets, Relational Contracting* (New York: Free Press, 1985).

43. Early institutional theorists, such as Philip Selznick, emphasized administrators' commitments to norms. Subsequently, institutional theorists have tended to focus on cognitive rather than normative factors. See Paul J. DiMaggio and Walter W. Powell, "Introduction," in Walter W. Powell and Paul J. DiMaggio (eds.), *The New Institutionalism in Organizational Analysis* (Chicago: University of Chicago Press, 1991), 11–15. Scholars of culture

have more recently emphasized the role of norms. See Edgar H. Schein, "Culture: The Missing Concept in Organizational Studies," *Administrative Science Quarterly* 41, no. 2 (1996): 229–240; and Michael L. Tushman and Charles A. O'Reilly III, *Winning through Innovation* (Boston: Harvard Business School Press, 1997), especially 99–154.

44. Steven Klepper and Kenneth L. Simons have analyzed a large sample of early tire producers and demonstrated that investment in research and development is a statistically significant predictor of an entrant's likelihood of surviving the ultimate shakeout in the tire sector. See Steven Klepper and Kenneth L. Simons, "The Making of an Oligopoly: Firm Survival and Technological Change in the Evolution of the U.S. Tire Industry," *Journal of Political Economy* 108, no. 4 (2000): 728–760.

45. Steve Love and David Giffels, *Wheels of Fortune: The Story of Rubber in Akron* (Akron, OH: University of Akron Press, 1999), 152.

CHAPTER TWO

1. Alan Meyer defines the construct of environmental jolt as "a sudden and unprecedented event . . . whose occurrence [is] difficult to foresee and whose impact on an organization [is] disruptive and potentially inimical." See Alan D. Meyer, "Adapting to Environmental Jolts," *Administrative Science Quarterly* 27 (1982): 515. Not every shift in a firm's context is a dramatic jolt, however, and it would be interesting to develop a more comprehensive taxonomy of environmental shifts.

2. Donald N. Sull, "Why Good Companies Go Bad," *Harvard Business Review,* July–August 1999; and Donald N. Sull, "The Dynamics of Standing Still," *Business History Review* 73, no. 3 (1999): 430–464.

3. This passive framing of inertia is consistent with the population ecology literature. Michael Hannan and John H. Freeman defined structural inertia in the following terms: "[S]tructures of organizations have high inertia when the speed of reorganization [change in core features] is much lower than the rate at which environmental conditions change." Michael Hannan and John H. Freeman, "Structural Inertia and Organizational Change," *American Sociological Review* 49 (1984): 151. Structural inertia, according to population ecologists, implies that organizations make adaptive changes but do so too slowly. Active inertia, in contrast, suggests that managers often respond quite promptly to major changes in their competitive environment. The failure of organizations to adapt, in this view, results not from delay in action, but from inappropriate action. The maladaptive response results from the constraints that historical commitments place on an organization's actions.

4. See Anthony Giddens, *Central Problems in Social Theory: Action, Structure and Contradictions in Social Analysis* (London: Macmillan, 1979), and Anthony Giddens, *The Constitution of Society: Outline of the Theory of Structuration* (Berkeley: University of California Press, 1984).

5. Dorothy Leonard introduced a second duality of structure in her influential article, "Core Capabilities and Core Rigidities: A Paradox in Managing New Product Development," *Strategic Management Journal* 13 (1992): 111–125. Leonard uses the term *core capabilities* to describe an organization's structure and argues that core capabilities in new product and process development simultaneously enhance development in dominant research disciplines while inhibiting development in nondominant disciplines. Giddens's notion of duality illuminates the interaction between agents and enduring structures. Leonard's, in contrast, focuses attention on the interaction between enduring structures and an organization's competitive environment. These two notions of duality are distinctive but complementary, and I draw upon both in my model.

6. The construct of structure can be used at different levels of analysis. Societies have structures, as do industries, firms, or subunits within an organization (e.g., divisions, functional departments). In using the notion of structure, therefore, we must clearly answer: "At what level of analysis are we applying this construct?" The success formula implicitly focuses on structure at the level of an organization as a whole, between its competitive environment and the individual agents—specifically, entrepreneurs and managers—who make commitments.

In situating the organizational context between the external competitive environment and the individual agents, I follow the precedent of Stewart Ranson, C. R. Hinings, and Royston Greenwood, "The Structuring of Organizational Structures," *Administrative Science Quarterly* 25 (1980): 1–17, and Andrew M. Pettigrew, *The Awakening Giant: Continuity and Change in Imperial Chemical Industries* (Oxford: Blackwell, 1985). Richard Whittington rightly points out that situating structure at the organizational level of analysis (and thereby omitting analysis of other social structures) sacrifices some of the richness of Giddens's theory. See Richard Whittington, "Putting Giddens into Action: Social Systems and Managerial Agency," *Journal of Management Studies* 29, no. 6 (1992): 693–712. I agree, but also note that an attempt to simultaneously incorporate all structures into a single framework would render that model intractable as a tool for analyzing the evolution of structure over time.

7. For references to the term "quantum organization," see Danny Miller and Peter H. Friesen, *Organizations: A Quantum View* (Englewood

Cliffs, NJ: Prentice Hall, 1984); for "deep structure," see Michael L. Tushman and Elaine Romanelli, "Organizational Evolution: A Metamorphosis Model of Convergence and Reorientation," in L. L. Cummings and Barry M. Staw (eds.), *Research in Organizational Behavior* (Greenwich, CT: JAI Press, 1985), 171–222, and Connie J. G. Gersick, "Revolutionary Change Theories: A Multilevel Exploration of the Punctuated Equilibrium Paradigm," *Academy of Management Review* 16, no. 1 (1991): 10–36; for "archetypes," see Royston Greenwood and C. R. Hinings, "Understanding Strategic Change: The Contribution of Archetypes," *Academy of Management Journal* 36, no. 5 (1993): 1052–1081; and for "institution," see John W. Meyer and Brian Rowan, "Institutionalized Organizations: Formal Structure as Myth and Ceremony," *American Journal of Sociology* 83 (1977): 340–363.

8. For an excellent critique of Giddens's specification of structure, see William H. Sewell, Jr., "A Theory of Structure: Duality, Agency and Transformation," *American Journal of Sociology* 98 (1992): 1–29.

9. To structure the process of iterating between my findings and the literature, I created a matrix of prominent theories of inertia. Each column in the matrix represented a stream of theory, and the cells in the column listed the factors that contributed to inertia according to that theory. I then arranged the cells into rows of approximately similar categories that were sufficiently broad to subsume the factors specified by existing models.

I had three objectives in selecting the final categories for inclusion in the success formula. First, I attempted to achieve internal validity by ensuring the conceptual categories accurately explained the data I observed in my initial and most in-depth case studies in the tire industry. Second, I tried to achieve external validity by developing a set of categories that were useful in understanding the sources of inertia in the other companies in my sample. Third, I worked to develop a framework that would be useful to practitioners.

The objective of managerial usefulness had important implications for my selection of categories. Normative theory should be parsimonious, in my opinion, because managers are more likely to understand, remember, and act upon a simple theory than a complex model. This implies a small number of broad categories (five in my model) versus a large number of narrow categories that might be appropriate for a statistical model. My desire for useful theory also led me to favor categories that managers could grasp intuitively (e.g., processes, relationships) over more abstract constructs such as dynamic capabilities. I am grateful to Professor Michael E. Porter, who clarified the importance of selecting intuitive variables in building frameworks that managers can use.

2. Extensive empirical literature provides evidence that financial performance in excess of the industry average decreases the likelihood that firms will reorient their strategy, even in the face of a discontinuous change in the environment. See Frances J. Milliken and Theresa K. Lant, "The Effect of an Organization's Recent Performance History on Strategic Persistence and Change: The Role of Managerial Interpretations," in P. Shrivastava, A. Huff, and J. E. Dutton (eds.), *Advances in Strategic Management*, Volume 7 (Greenwich, CT: JAI Press, 1991), 129–156, and Henrich R. Greve, "Performance Aspirations and Risky Organizational Change," *Administrative Science Quarterly* 43 (1998): 58–86. For a clear discussion of the individual psychological processes that mediate the relationship between organizational success and managers' decisions that contribute to persistence in the face of environmental change, see Pino G. Audia, Edwin A. Locke, and Ken G. Smith, "The Paradox of Success: An Archival and a Laboratory Study of Strategic Persistence Following Radical Environmental Change," *Academy of Management Journal* 43, no. 5 (2000): 837–853. Audia et al. identify several psychological processes that link superior performance to persistence: Satisfaction with performance, confidence in the effectiveness of the current formula, managers' confidence in their ability to execute specific tasks well, goals, and the amount and type of information sought by managers. I would add to this list a financial link. Superior performance provides the financial capital that allows a company to avoid the discipline of submitting their subsequent investment decisions to the scrutiny of potential investors when seeking outside funding. Danny Miller has argued that success tends to simplify an organization's structure, which deprives managers of alternatives and increases their attachment to the existing frames, values, and processes. See Danny Miller, "The Architecture of Simplicity," *Academy of Management Review* 18, no. 1 (1993): 116–138. My research provided limited support for this hypothesis, since several of the companies in my sample, including Daewoo, Samsung, Lloyds TSB, and National Westminster, pursued a success formula that included diversification.

3. Stock performance calculated as the value of one dollar invested in either the stock or the relevant index, with returns adjusted for splits and corporate share repurchases. Dividends assumed reinvested in the company's stock. Beginning date for each comparison is publication date for issue. End date for all is 10 October 2002, except for the companies that delisted because of merger or acquisition—their stock performance is calculated to the date of delisting. Underperformance is defined as performance at least 10 percent lower than the benchmark index. If the cutoff for underperformance were set 5 percent lower than the benchmark, six of the seven

companies would have underperformed. Data on CEO exits prior to retirement date from various issues of the *Wall Street Journal*.

4. Circulation data from Audit Bureau of Circulations.

5. Jerry Flint and Julie Pitta, "Defeating the Cover Jinx," *Forbes,* 12 January 1998, 95.

6. Chao C. Chen and James R. Meindl, "The Construction of Leadership Images in the Popular Press: The Case of Donald Burr and People Express," *Administrative Science Quarterly* 36, no. 4 (1991): 521–555.

7. See Rakesh Khurana, *Searching for a Corporate Savior: The Irrational Quest for Charismatic CEOs* (Princeton: Princeton University Press, 2002).

8. Mathew Hayward and Donald Hambrick argue that favorable media attention contributes to managers' inflated sense of self-confidence, which leads them to overpay for acquisitions. In their study of 106 large acquisitions, they find that favorable press coverage is highly correlated with large premiums paid for acquisitions. See Mathew L. A. Hayward and Donald C. Hambrick, "Explaining the Premiums Paid for Large Acquisitions: Evidence of CEO Hubris," *Administrative Science Quarterly* 42 (1997): 103–127.

9. Polybius, *Histories,* translated by W. R. Paton, (Cambridge, MA: Loeb Classical Library, 1954).

10. See Jacqueline de Romilly, *The Rise and Fall of States According to Greek Authors* (Ann Arbor, MI: University of Michigan Press, 1997).

11. Several good translations of Thucydides are in print. Steven Lattimore's translation (Indianapolis: Hackett, 1998) converts Thucydides' challenging Greek into accessible English and incorporates recent scholarship on Thucydides.

12. Thucydides, ibid., v. 89.

13. Alfred Marshall, *Principles of Economics* (1890; reprint, London: Macmillan, 1966).

14. The two stadiums were Buffalo's Rich Stadium, named in 1973 after the Rich Products Corporation, and the Great Western Forum—which hosted the Los Angeles Lakers and was named after the Great Western Bank in 1987. Both were subsequently renamed. The Chicago Cubs' Wrigley Field and St. Louis Cardinals' Busch Stadium were both named after individuals—William Wrigley Jr. and Augustus Busch Jr.—rather than the companies that bore their names. See Larry M. McCarthy and Richard Irwin, "Names in Lights: Corporate Purchase of Sport Facility Naming Rights," *The Cyber-Journal of Sport Marketing,* 21 June 1998.

15. Kim Woo-Choong, *Every Street Is Paved with Gold* (New York: William Morrow, 1992). The original book was published in Korean in 1989 under the title *It's a Big World and There Is Lots to Be Done.*

16. See Rosabeth Moss Kanter, *Men and Women of the Corporation* (New York: Basic Books, 1977).

17. Irving Janis introduced the term "groupthink" to describe a team's convergence on a single viewpoint. See Irving L. Janis, *Victims of Groupthink* (Boston: Houghton Mifflin, 1972). An extensive body of literature has examined how the demographic characteristics (e.g., organizational tenure, industry tenure, age) of top executives influence the decisions they make. For an excellent review of the literature on top management teams, see Sydney Finkelstein and Donald C. Hambrick, *Strategic Leadership: Top Executives and Their Effects on Organizations* (Minneapolis, MN: West, 1996), particularly 115–161. Donald Hambrick and his colleagues have examined in particular how a top management team's demographic characteristics influence their state of attachment to the status quo. See Donald C. Hambrick, Marta A. Geletkanycz, and James W. Frederickson, "Top Executive Commitment to the Status Quo: Some Tests of Its Determinants," *Strategic Management Journal* 14 (1993): 401–418. Their study found that tenure in an industry was strongly correlated with managers' attachment to the status quo and also that incumbent managers tended to believe that their successors should be like them. This stream of research has provided valuable insights into how the top managers' characteristics influence their decisions. It has paid less attention to how managers' actions, such as public promises or statements, influence their subsequent decisions.

18. As of August 1998, "Power Elites of Top 5 Groups," *Shindonga,* November 1998, in Korean.

19. Donald N. Sull, "From Community of Innovation to Community of Inertia: The Rise and Fall of the Akron Tire Industry," working paper 01–025, Harvard Business School, Boston, 2001.

20. Michael Porter defines an industrial cluster as "a geographically proximate group of interconnected companies and associated institutions in a particular field, linked by commonalities and complementarities." Michael E. Porter, "Clusters and Competition: New Agendas for Companies, Governments, and Institutions," in Michael E. Porter (ed.), *On Competition* (Boston: Harvard Business School Press, 1998), 199. Economists have argued that geographic colocation allows the concentration of supporting institutions and specialized inputs and also enables the transfer of specialized knowledge across firms within the cluster. See Porter, "Clusters and

Competition," and Paul R. Krugman, "Increasing Returns and Economic Geography," *Journal of Political Economy* 99, no. 3 (1991): 483–499. Institutional theory suggests that geographic clustering can increase the legitimacy of constituent firms and increase their ability to secure required resources. See Howard E. Aldrich and C. Marlene Fiol, "Fools Rush In? The Institutional Context of Industry Creation," *Academy of Management Review* 19, no. 4 (1994): 645–670. Although the benefits of clustering are often viewed in static terms, they can change over time. The value of shared knowledge in promoting technical innovation, to take one example, can decrease as an industry converges on a dominant design. See Sull, "From Community of Innovation to Community of Inertia."

CHAPTER FOUR

1. Data on Asahi Breweries from company annual reports and financial statements, various years; Jiru Kokuryo, Shigeru Asaba, and Malcolm S. Salter, "Asahi Breweries, Ltd.," Case 389-114 (Boston: Harvard Business School, 1994); and Timothy J. Craig, "Resource Development in Firms: New Product Development and Organizational Change in the Japanese Brewing Industry" (Ph.D. diss., University of Washington, 1992).

2. Financial performance calculated as Asahi's returns from the period that Asahi Dry was introduced through February 2002 compared to the Japanese Brewers stock price index. Performance adjusted to account for stock splits and share repurchases. Dividends were assumed reinvested in the stock. Performance calculated at end of month. Data from Datastream International.

3. See Terry L. Amburgey, Dawn Kelly, and William P. Barnett, "Resetting the Clock: The Dynamics of Organizational Change and Failure," *Administrative Science Quarterly* 38 (1993): 51–73.

4. See for example, Mark Halper et al., "Are You Next: 20 Industries That Must Change," *Business 2.0*, March 1999.

5. Robert Burgelman argues that promising alternatives to a company's traditional business often emerge outside its core business. See Robert A. Burgelman, "Fading Memories: A Process Theory of Strategic Business Exit in Dynamic Environments," *Administrative Science Quarterly* 39 (1994): 24–56.

6. The "law of requisite variety" states that a system's internal variety must match the level of variety found in its environment. See W. Ross Ashby, *An Introduction to Cybernetics* (London: Chapman & Hall, 1970).

7. I am grateful to Professor Erwin Daneels for bringing the Smith-Corona case to my attention. Data on Smith-Corona is taken primarily from

an interview with John A. Bermingham, president and CEO of Smith-Corona, that appeared in the *Wall Street Transcript*, 15 November 1999, and from the corporate history on the company's Web site.

8. Clayton M. Christensen, *The Innovator's Dilemma: When New Technologies Cause Great Firms to Fail* (Boston: Harvard Business School Press, 1997). In an intriguing study of newspapers' response to the Internet, Clark Gilbert finds that the newspaper managers who framed the Internet as a threat to their core business were able to mobilize resources for their own online businesses. The threat framing, however, led to rigidity in the newspaper companies' resource allocation process that blunted the effectiveness of their response. See Clark G. Gilbert, "Can Competing Frames Co-exist: The Paradox of Threatened Response," working paper 02-056, Harvard Business School, Boston, 2002.

9. I am grateful to Kirsten Sandberg for first suggesting this metaphor and to Linda Cyr for helping me understand the technicalities of rock climbing.

10. Data on IBM's transformation from Louis V. Gerstner, *Who Says Elephants Can't Dance: Inside IBM's Historic Turnaround* (New York: HarperBusiness, 2002); Robert Slater, *Saving Big Blue: Leadership Lessons and Turnaround Tactics of IBM's Lou Gerstner* (New York: McGraw-Hill, 1999); Doug Garr, *IBM Redux: Lou Gerstner and the Business Turnaround of the Decade* (New York: HarperBusiness, 1999); Robert D. Austin and Richard L. Nolan, "IBM Corporation Turnaround," Case 600-098 (Boston: Harvard Business School, 1998); IBM annual reports, various years; and articles from the business press.

11. Jim Carlton, *Apple: The Inside Story of Intrigue, Egomania, and Business Blunders* (New York: Times Business/Random House, 1997); Owen W. Linzmayer, *Apple Confidential: The Real Story of Apple Computer, Inc.* (San Francisco: No Starch Press, 1999); and Michael S. Malone (Michael Shawn), *Infinite Loop: How the World's Most Insanely Great Computer Company Went Insane* (New York: Currency/Doubleday, 1999).

12. Steven Burke, "Mike Spindler," *Computer Reseller News*, 14 November 1994, 123.

CHAPTER FIVE

1. Donald N. Sull and David A. Garvin, "Pepsi's Regeneration, 1990–1993," Case 395-048 (Boston: Harvard Business School, 1994).

2. Sull and Garvin, "Pepsi's Regeneration, 1990–1993," 3–4.

3. Data sources on the Nokia story include Dan Steinbock, *The Nokia Revolution* (New York: American Management Association, 2001), and Katherine Doornik and John Roberts, "Nokia Corporation: Innovation and

Efficiency in a High-Growth Global Firm," Case S-IB-23 (Stanford, CA: Stanford Business School, 2001). Although I conducted extensive interviews at Nokia, I did not publish a case study, and all of the data reported in this section is available in public sources.

4. These questions were posed to Scandinavian consumers in a Nokia advertising campaign in the late 1980s. See Steinbock, *The Nokia Revolution,* 53.

5. Data on Samsung from Donald N. Sull, Simon Andrews, Sam Baker, and Lee Ji-Hwan, "Driving Ambition: Samsung's Entry into the Automotive Market," Case CS98-02 (London: London Business School, 1998), and Park Choelsoon and Donald N. Sull, "The Rise and Fall of Korean *Chaebols*: Daewoo and Samsung," working paper, Seoul National University, Seoul, 2002.

6. Data from Korea Listed Companies Association. Advertising and revenue figures for the five largest divisions in the Samsung Group— that is, electronics, heavy industry, SDI, electromechanics, and Samsung Techwin.

7. Data from U.S. Patent and Trademark Office.

8. Search conducted by the author on October 12, 2001.

9. David A. Garvin has conducted a thorough and comprehensive analysis of organizational processes, including how managers use nonoperating processes to transform their organization. See David A. Garvin, "The Processes of Organization and Management," *Sloan Management Review,* Summer 1998, for a summary of his findings; and David A. Garvin, *General Management: Processes and Action* (New York: Irwin/McGraw Hill, 2001), for a more in-depth overview. Garvin's case study on Harvey Golub's transformation of American Express by using decision processes is a particularly rich example. See David A. Garvin and Artemis March, "Harvey Golub: Recharging American Express," Case 396-212 (Boston: Harvard Business School, 1996).

10. Data for Duck-Yang case from Kim Ki-Chan, Donald N. Sull, and Sirh Jin-Young, *Strategic Transformation Through Quality* (Seoul: Seoul National University Press, 1998).

11. Data on Xerox from Beatriz Guimaraes, "Xerox: The Road to Reconstruction," London Business School, unpublished Sloan master's thesis, 1998.

12. David T. Kearns and David A. Nadler, *Prophets in the Dark* (New York: HarperBusiness, 1992); and Gary Jacobson and John Hillkirk, *Xerox: American Samurai* (New York: Collier, 1986).

13. Douglas K. Smith and Robert C. Alexander, *Fumbling the Future: How Xerox Invented, Then Ignored the First Personal Computer* (New York: Morrow, 1988).

14. John Seely Brown and Paul Duguid, *The Social Life of Information* (Boston: Harvard Business School Press, 2000).

15. Kavita Abraham and Sumantra Ghoshal, "Infosys Technologies Limited: Going Global," in Sumantra Ghoshal, Gita Piramal, and Sudeep Budhiraja (eds.), *World Class in India* (New Delhi: Penguin Books India, 2001), 618–639. See also William J. Coughlin and Walter Kuemmerle, "Infosys: Financing an Indian Software Start-up," Case 9-800-103 (Boston: Harvard Business School, 2000).

16. Data on Lloyds TSB drawn primarily from interviews with Lloyds TSB executives. Supplemental sources include corporate annual reports and published financials, various years; articles from the business press; Junko Matsumi, *Transformation of Established and Bureaucratic Organizations: Lloyds TSB and NatWest,* London Business School, unpublished Sloan master's thesis, 2002; and David Rogers, *The Big Four British Banks: Organization, Strategy and the Future* (New York: St. Martin's Press, 1999).

17. Data on Nikko Securities drawn primarily from interviews with executives. I am very grateful to Masako Egawa, executive director of the Harvard Business School Japan Research Office, for arranging the interviews. Supplemental sources include Ned Akov, "Nikko Cordial Corporation," *ING Barings Equity Research,* 25 March 2002; Walter Altherr, "Nikko Securities," *CSFB Equity Research,* 13 April 2001; Nikko Cordial annual reports, various years; and articles from the business press.

18. Michael L. Tushman and Elaine Romanelli, "Organizational Evolution: A Metamorphosis Model of Convergence and Reorientation," in Lawrence L. Cummings and Barry M. Staw (eds.), *Research in Organizational Behavior* (Greenwich, CT: JAI Press, 1985), 171–222.

19. I am deeply indebted to Christopher D. McKenna for drawing my attention to McKinsey's formative years as a successful example of values as an anchor. I have drawn on preliminary drafts from his forthcoming book on the history of the management consulting industry, particularly chapter 7. Additional resources include two books by Marvin Bower, *The Development of Executive Leadership* (Cambridge, MA: Harvard University Press, 1949), and *The Will to Lead: Running a Business with a Network of Leaders* (Boston: Harvard Business School Press, 1997). My understanding of McKinsey was also informed by my time as a consultant with the firm during the late 1980s.

CHAPTER SIX

1. See Donald N. Sull, "The Dynamics of Standing Still: Firestone Tire & Rubber and the Radial Revolution," *Business History Review* 73 (1999): 430–464.

2. From "The Gambler," written by Don Schlitz, ©1978.

3. For a comprehensive review of the executive succession literature, see Idalene F. Kesner and Terrence C. Sebora, "Executive Succession: Past, Present and Future," *Journal of Management* 20, no. 2 (1994): 327–372.

4. Andrew S. Grove, *Only the Paranoid Survive: How to Exploit the Crisis Points That Challenge Every Company and Career* (New York: Harper Collins Business, 1996), 81–97, and Robert A. Burgelman, "Fading Memories: A Process Theory of Strategic Business Exit in Dynamic Environments," *Administrative Science Quarterly* 39, no. 1 (1994): 24–56.

5. Shell example from Misha Shukov, Sandor Talas, and Donald N. Sull, "Royal Dutch/Shell: Retail Transformation in Hungary," Case CS98-03 (London: London Business School, 1998).

6. For an excellent study of how rhetoric can spur action, see Robert G. Eccles and Nitin Nohria, *Beyond the Hype: Rediscovering the Essence of Management* (Boston: Harvard Business School Press, 1992). For an accessible and useful guide for managers trying to improve their own rhetoric, see Jay Conger, *Winning 'Em Over* (New York: Simon & Schuster, 1998).

7. This section draws on an article I wrote entitled "The Rhetoric of Transformation," *Financial Times Mastering Management Review* 30 (December 1999): 34–37. The data on Jack Welch's rhetoric comes from Jack Welch, "Letter to the Shareholders," General Electric Company annual reports, 1989–2000. Eduardo Tubosaka provided a valuable analysis of the history of Welch's commitments in his unpublished master's thesis at the London Business School.

8. Lloyd Bitzer, "The Rhetorical Situation," *Philosophy and Rhetoric*, January 1968, 1–14.

CHAPTER SEVEN

1. Various research streams distinguish between the object of commitment and actions that increase its effectiveness. Speech act theory, for example, distinguishes between what is committed to (e.g., the truth of an expressed proposition, a future course of action) and the illocutionary force of the commitment, which refers to how strongly a specific speech act commits the speaker. See J. L. Austin, *How to Do Things with Words* (Oxford: Oxford University Press, 1962), and John R. Searle, *Speech Acts* (Cambridge, UK: Cambridge University Press, 1969). Game theorists also distin-

guish between the object of commitment and its credibility. For a nontechnical overview, see David M. Kreps, *Game Theory and Economic Modeling* (Oxford: Oxford University Press, 1990).

2. Data for Oticon comes from Mette Morsing and Kristian Eiberg (eds.), *Managing the Unmanageable for a Decade* (Hellerup, Denmark: Oticon, 1998); John J. Kao, "Oticon," Case 395-144 (Boston: Harvard Business School, 1995); Bjorn Lovas and Sumantra Ghoshal, "Strategy as Guided Evolution," *Strategic Management Journal* 21, no. 9 (2000): 875–896; and interviews by the author with Oticon managers.

3. In his initial memo outlining his plan to transform Oticon, Kolind lists the purchasing, sales, and administration processes as targets for a shift to project-based management in addition to new product development. New product development, however, was clearly his focal process. See Lars Kolind, "How Will Oticon Look in the Future?" Oticon internal memorandum dated December 1989 in Morsing and Eiberg, *Managing the Unmanageable for a Decade,* 20–25. For a broader discussion of organizational transformation through a commitment to the new product development process, see Steven C. Wheelwright and Kim B. Clark, *Revolutionizing New Product Development* (New York: Free Press, 1992).

4. Thomas Schelling provided an early and comprehensive overview of the role of credible commitments when agents must coordinate their actions to achieve a mutually desired goal. See Thomas C. Schelling, *The Strategy of Conflict* (Cambridge, MA: Harvard University Press, 1960), especially 83–118. Jon Elster introduces a taxonomy of three broad categories of mechanisms by which agents can render a precommitment credible. See Jon Elster, *Ulysses and the Sirens: Studies in Rationality and Irrationality* (Cambridge, UK: Cambridge University Press, 1979). First, agents can manipulate the feasible set of future alternatives or modify the incentives associated with pursuing alternative courses of action. This category is the focus of most economists' analysis of commitments. Elster also argues that agents can manipulate their character over time periods by proactively changing their preference structure. I discussed the link between personal character and transforming commitments in chapter 6. Finally, Elster argues that agents can actively manipulate their information set by avoiding exposure to certain signals. We could catalog all the mechanisms that lend credibility; but, ultimately, multiple factors influence an agent's subjective assessment of how another agent will act in the future.

5. Industrial organization economists have thoroughly examined the role of credible commitments in influencing the behavior of competitors in product markets. Credible commitments also provide an alternative focal

point around which a new alignment of strategic frames, resources, processes, relationships, and values can emerge.

6. Scholars have tended to frame clarity of a commitment exclusively as a mechanism for increasing its credibility. Salancik, for example, lists "explicitness" as one of four determinants of the degree of credibility (the other three are revocability, volition, and public-ness of the act). Gerald R. Salancik, "Commitment and the Control of Organizational Behavior and Belief," in Barry M. Staw and Gerald R. Salancik (eds.), *New Directions in Organizational Behavior* (Chicago: St. Clair Press, 1977). Salancik argues that explicitness matters because it allows outside observers to monitor and assess whether a promised action has indeed been executed.

7. Saying attributed to Oliver Wendell Holmes.

CHAPTER EIGHT

1. Rakesh Khurana argues that directors frequently bypass qualified internal candidates in an irrational search for a charismatic outside CEO. See Rakesh Khurana, *Searching for a Corporate Savior: The Irrational Quest for Charismatic CEOs* (Princeton, NJ: Princeton University Press, 2002). While I agree with Khurana's core argument, I believe that boards' search for outsiders may also be motivated by the desire to find candidates with previous experience leading a transformation. Success in conspicuous turnarounds, such as Gerstner's experience at RJR Nabisco prior to joining IBM, would, of course, attract the media coverage associated with charisma. In some circumstances, directors might quite rationally believe that the benefits of transformation experience outweigh the costs of incomplete understanding of the company and industry.

2. Gil Amelio and William L. Simon, *Profit from Experience: The National Semiconductor Story of Transformation Management* (New York: Van Nostrand Reinhold, 1996); Gil Amelio and William L. Simon, *On the Firing Line: My 500 Days at Apple* (New York: HarperBusiness, 1998); Jim Carlton, *Apple: The Inside Story of Intrigue, Egomania, and Business Blunders* (New York: Times Business/Random House, 1997); Alan Deutschman, *The Second Coming of Steve Jobs* (New York: Broadway Books, 2000); Owen W. Linzmayer, *Apple Confidential: The Real Story of Apple Computer, Inc.* (San Francisco: No Starch Press, 1999); and Michael S. Malone, *Infinite Loop: How the World's Most Insanely Great Computer Company Went Insane* (New York: Currency/Doubleday, 1999).

3. Patricia Sellers, "Can Chainsaw Al Really Be a Builder?" *Fortune*, 12 January 1998; Martha Brannigan and James R. Hagerty, "Chain-Sawed: Sunbeam, Its Prospects Looking Ever Worse, Fires CEO Dunlap—Cost-

Cutter Extraordinaire Failed to Deliver Results He Had Long Promised," *Wall Street Journal*, 15 June 1998; John A. Byrne, "How Al Dunlap Self-destructed: The Inside Story of What Drove Sunbeam's Board to Act," *Business Week*, 6 July 1998; John A. Byrne, "Chainsaw: He Anointed Himself America's Best CEO. But Al Dunlap Drove Sunbeam into the Ground," *Business Week*, 18 October 1999; Albert J. Dunlap, *Mean Business: How I Save Bad Companies and Make Good Companies Great* (New York: Times Business, 1996).

4. Joann Muller, "Kmart's Last Chance: Can Adamson Fill the Talent Gap That Has Plagued the Chain?" *Business Week*, 11 March 2002; Amy Merrick, "Kmart Lays Out Plans to Trim Its Size, Increase Efficiency in Bankruptcy Filing," *Wall Street Journal*, 23 January 2002; Joann Muller and Ann Therese Palmer, "Kmart's Bright Idea: Can Revamped Stores and the Revival of the Blue Light Special Bring Back Customers and Profits?" *Business Week*, 9 April 2001.

5. The Enron story has been extensively documented. For good overviews of the successful aspects of Enron's transformation see Agis Salpukas, "Firing Up an Idea Machine: Enron Is Encouraging the Entrepreneurs Within," *New York Times*, 27 June 1999; and Harry Hurt, III, "Power Players," *Fortune*, 5 August 1996.

6. Joseph L. Bower, *Managing the Resource Allocation Process: A Study of Corporate Planning and Investment* (Boston: Harvard Business School Press, 1970).

7. Ken Brown and Ianthe Jeanne Dugan, "Sad Account: Andersen's Fall from Grace Is a Tale of Greed and Miscues—Pushed to Boost Revenue, Auditors Acted as Sellers, Warred with Consultants," *Wall Street Journal*, 7 June 2002; John A. Byrne, "Fall from Grace: Joe Berardino Presided Over the Biggest Accounting Scandals Ever and the Demise of a Legendary Firm," *Business Week*, 12 August 2002; and Ashish Nanda and Scott Landry, "Family Feud (A): Andersen v. Andersen," Case 9-800-064 (Boston: Harvard Business School, 2000).

8. Mark Landler, "The Fraternity of Corporate Exiles: Europe Executives Undone," *New York Times*, 30 July 2002; Matthew Karnitschnig and Neal E. Boudette, "History Lesson: Battle for the Soul of Bertelsmann Led to CEO Ouster," *Wall Street Journal*, 30 July 2002; and Martin Peers, Matthew Rose, and Matthew Karnitschnig, "At Bertelsmann, Another Blow to Futuristic Media Visions—Middlehoff's Exit Spotlights Failure of Expensive Bets on Electronic Businesses," *Wall Street Journal*, 29 July 2002.

9. Data on Compaq from Richard Coffey, Tracey Luke, and Donald N. Sull, "Compaq at a Crossroads," Case CS99-01 (London: London Business

School, 1999); Jason E. Green and William A. Sahlman, "Benjamin Rosen and Compaq," Case 296-002 (Boston: Harvard Business School, 1995); and Alan M. Webber, "Consensus, Continuity, and Common Sense: An Interview with Compaq's Rod Canion," *Harvard Business Review*, July–August 1990; and corporate annual reports and published financials, various years.

10. Stock price performance data of Compaq versus NASDAQ from Datastream.

Donald N. Sull is an Assistant Professor at Harvard Business School, where he studies how managers transform companies to respond effectively to changes in their competitive environment. He also serves as an adviser to firms in the United States, Europe, and Asia. Before entering academia, he worked as a consultant with McKinsey & Company and as a member of the management team that restructured the Uniroyal-Goodrich Tire Company.

Sull has won awards including the George S. Dively Award for outstanding dissertation, the Newcomen Prize for the best paper in business history, and inclusion in the Academy of Management Best Paper Proceedings. He received his A.B., M.B.A., and doctorate from Harvard University.

Sull lives in Newton, Massachusetts, with his wife, Theresa, and their four children.